The National Computing Centre develops techniques, provides services, offers aids and supplies information to encourage the more effective use of Information Technology. The Centre co-operates with members and other organisations, including government bodies, to develop the use of computers and communications facilities. It provides advice, training and consultancy; evaluates software methods and tools; promotes standards and codes of practice; and publishes books.

Any interested company, organisation or individual can benefit from the work of the Centre – by exploring its products and services; or in particular by subscribing as a member. Throughout the country, members can participate in working parties, study groups and discussions; and can influence NCC policy.

For more information, contact the Centre at Oxford Road, Manchester M1 7ED (061-228 6333), or at one of the regional offices: London (01-353 4875), Bristol (0272-277 077), Birmingham (021-236 6283), Glasgow (041-204 1101) or Belfast (0232-665 997).

NCC THE
NATIONAL CENTRE
FOR INFORMATION
TECHNOLOGY

Computer Weekly (Reed Business Publishing, Quadrant House, Sutton, Surrey, SM2 5AS) provides news, reviews and features for its circulation of over 112,000 computer professionals each week. Computer Weekly Publications is the book publishing arm of *Computer Weekly* newspaper and publishes books relevant to and of interest to the computer industry.

Selling Information Technology

A Practical Career Guide

Eric Johnson

PUBLISHED BY NCC PUBLICATIONS

British Library Cataloguing in Publication Data

Johnson, Eric
    Selling information technology:
    a practical career guide.
    1. Computer systems. Marketing
    I. Title
    004′.068′8

    ISBN 0-85012-684-3

First published in 1989 by:

NCC Publications, The National Computing Centre Limited, Oxford Road, Manchester M1 7ED, England.

Typeset in 10pt Souvenir ITC Light by Bookworm Typesetting, Manchester; and printed by Hobbs the Printers of Southampton.

ISBN 0-85012-684-3

Foreword

The key role played by those in the front line of the IT industry – the IT sales person – is often unsung. In this book Eric Johnson shows how the rapidly changing IT industry makes demands on its sales people which probably make them the most skilled in the profession of selling.

The IT sales person not only needs to understand users, hardware, software and applications, but also requires the skill and creativity to combine this understanding to sell solutions rather than boxes.

Computer Weekly and The National Computing Centre, which both aim to promote high standards of IT professionalism in all sectors of the industry, are proud to demonstrate their appreciation for the new role of the IT sales person in this unique collaboration.

We recognise that a highly professional and creative sales force is a positive force within the industry, and if this handbook for IT sales people helps in some small way to enhance this professionalism, our own collaboration will have been well worthwhile.

David Craver
Editor-in-Chief,
Computer Weekly

Geoff Simons
Managing Editor,
NCC Publications

Preface

When I was asked to write this book my first reaction was negative. Many excellent books on professional selling had already been published so why repeat the same message? Then I started to reflect on my own industry, information technology, which had been very good to me for over 30 years. This industry was complex, wide ranging in its application and rather unique. Its output pervaded every section of the economy. Moreover it was expanding at a faster rate than any other industry. The people who sold its products had to be rather special.

Having been involved in the IT evolution – from the unit accounting devices and punched cards of the 1950s through four generations of computing technology – perhaps I could channel some of this experience into a set of guidelines for the next generation of computer salespeople. The result is this book.

Today's IT salesman (and woman) is required to be a very professional person indeed. Not only is his/her client investing heavily in the IT product but the client could be dependent upon the IT solution for corporate survival. Thus the job demands a combination of knowledge and personal qualities which can be acquired or developed through dedicated learning and application. There is no room for failure but the rewards for success are high. For those wishing to accept this challenge this book is offered.

Acknowledgements

A book which attempts to guide people into a professional career is duty bound to provide the reader with a distillation of best practice as seen and experienced by the writer. Therefore I am indebted to my own organisation, The National Computing Centre Ltd, whose corporate objective includes that of attracting and retaining staff of the highest calibre and through which I have had the opportunity to practise and teach selling skills in the IT arena. I am especially grateful to Strategic Sales Training Ltd with which I have been closely involved in the training and development of NCC's sales and support team in recent years. Many of the principles involved in selling IT and proposed in Chapters 4 to 8 are taught by SST in its celebrated 'workshops', and through his book *Selling Professional Services* Tony Davis of SST offers a range of basic skills which I heartily recommend.

I shall always be thankful to NCR Ltd who gave me the chance to enter the sales profession over 30 years ago. The excellent sales methods which NCR taught me at the time were pioneered by the corporation's founders long before. I am pleased to say that I still apply them today.

I would also like to thank the following organisations for allowing me to reproduce some items, or to use their material, in the compilation of parts of the text:

Pedder Associates Ltd

Telecommunications Industry Research Centre

Manchester Polytechnic

The Times

Financial Times

Saville and Holdsworth Ltd

W B Saunders Company

Denis Crowe, Editor Top Pay Unit Review, *Income Data Services*

Computing

Finally my eternal gratitude to the word processing department at NCC, whose fine efforts produced the final draft.

Contents

Introduction

Outside the heady worlds of entertainment and sport, few careers offer such a high potential for self-expression and financial reward as does professional selling. The prosperity of thousands of companies, essential contributors to the wealth and well-being of the nation, depends ultimately on the skills and dedication of their salesforces.

Of course selling is but one of several corporate functions necessary for a business to grow and prosper. Research and development keep it ahead or at least abreast of the competition; manufacturing ensures products of the right quality; distribution channels ensure that the products will reach the market on time; planning and finance organise resources and keep things under control; and marketing – which includes the selling function – identifies opportunities and causes the development of products and services to meet such opportunities.

In the end though, it is all down to the salesman. He or she reflects the company's image and capability in the eye of the customer. Whether the customer chooses to do business with the company depends greatly on how it, and its products, are presented by the salesman. People who practise this social skill of selling, operate in virtually all sectors of the economy. They are the life blood of commerce. Their product portfolios range from financial services to motor cars, from fast-moving consumer goods to aircraft engines, from villas abroad to ethical drugs – the list is endless. Few however offer as much scope to the professional salesman as does the information technology industry.

Professor John Ashworth, Vice Chancellor of the University of Salford, has suggested, and most would agree, that IT has the potential to act as the most powerful motor of economic growth yet seen in the 20th Century.

"Being concerned with distribution of information, IT dramatically reverses the trend towards agglomeration that the Industrial Revolution set in train."

Clearly the IT industry has a golden future!

Some sources estimate that by the year 2000, two-thirds of all work will be *information* work. By 1995 it is estimated that between 4000 and 6000 billion dollars will be spent on electronic information equipment. Could the aspiring salesman ask for a better environment in which to practise his/her skills? I doubt it.

However the path to success in this business is far from easy. The successful salesman or woman will need to acquire a substantial understanding of business practice, organisational behaviour, computing technology and sales methods. He or she will also apply appropriate personal qualities to use this knowledge effectively in sales situations.

The object of this book is to provide the reader with an awareness of the characteristics of the IT industry, the markets it addresses, the requirements of its salespeople and the steps necessary to achieve a satisfying career. Throughout the text the word *salesman* will appear frequently. I would ask the reader to accept this as an all-embracing term, applying equally to sales*women*. Women have established themselves firmly in this profession and I have no doubt that they will continue to make a major contribution to its success.

Part 1
The Industry

Knowledge is of two kinds.
We know a subject ourselves, or
we know where we can find
information upon it.

— Dr Samuel Johnson

1 Information Technology

1.1 WHAT IT IS

1.1.1 Definition

Information Technology (IT) is the gathering, processing, interpretation and communication of information by means of computing technology. All work within an organisation generates, or uses information. In an office, typewriters or word processors generate information in the form of documents. Calculators manipulate information. Telephones transmit aural and vocal information. Photocopiers duplicate images of information. The procedures served by this information, and involved in gathering it, are all part of the organisation's Information System (IS).

Information systems were around long before computers were available to handle them, but the advent of IT has dramatically improved the accessibility of knowledge within information systems; the control and monitoring of business functions and staff creativity and performance. It can be argued that the organisation *is* the information system and *vice versa*. Certainly the way in which an IS functions will determine the success or otherwise of the organisation.

1.1.2 Converging Technologies

Office and computer technologies are converging. In today's office there is a wide range of equipment in use, all doing the same thing – processing information whether it be text, data or speech.

The change which is taking place is quite logical: it is the *convergence* of the separate elements of information processing to provide a unified approach – conceptually and physically – through multifunction equipment. One's view of 'information' is coloured by the way technologies have developed so far. Traditionally one thinks of *text* as letters or reports; *data* as computer terminal displays or printouts; *speech* as in telephone communication. But these categories can be extended. For example text can include telexes, reports, reference manuals, books and price lists. With IT these different ways of communicating information are becoming indistinct. The convergence of *word processing* is a combination of text handling and computer power which previously would have been directed towards data rather than text; *electronic mail* overlaps the traditional area of telex, letter writing, word processing and computing; and voice and data can now be combined on a single network simultaneously.

Information technology is happening *now* because the appropriate technology is relatively recent; the previous technology was too expensive but the silicon chip, digital data networks and fibre optics have changed all that. Previously there were insufficient incentives for individual suppliers. There is now potential for high rewards for those suppliers who work together at the point where the market is otherwise saturated with their individual devices.

There was less desire to link pieces of computer equipment together a few years ago and the needs of the purchaser were less sophisticated. Now there is an increasing demand for compatibility and standardisation from purchasers no longer prepared to be tied to one supplier.

1.2 IT'S IMPACT ON BUSINESS

1.2.1 Traditional Uses

Until recently computers have been used by the business community almost exclusively in a *defensive* fashion to cut costs and to minimise time taken to perform tasks. Cost justification was paramount. Few systems were purchased unless either staff levels could be reduced or administration processes streamlined.

1.2.2 Creative Uses

Now the fast developing attitude to computer usage is more *aggressive*. Computers are being used to increase the competitiveness of the user organisation, add value to its existing products and services, and help create new products and services. Such moves are designed to reposition the user's business in a new type of economy, an *information* economy, where the gathering and interpretation of information about the work of the organisation are as important to success (even survival) as its trading products or services. Properly implemented, IT can provide better, faster and more widely available information and the means to use it; improve communication with people inside and outside the organisation; and act as a vehicle of change. Above all computers can now be applied to change the *manner* in which companies *trade*.

In the past, computing technology was mostly used to process transactions which resulted from their method of trading. IT is now used by progressive businesses to help them protect their market from competition; make it attractive for customers to stay with them; create new market niches and add value to existing accounts; offer greater price flexibility; and generate new products through linking with other organisations.

1.2.3 Justification

IT is somewhat unique. Its hardware costs are decreasing whilst its capabilities and therefore potential benefits are improving, and its rival costs such as salaries, wages and office supplies are increasing. Surely this is a formula to reduce operating costs.

Traditionally IT is justified on a Return on Investment (ROI) basis, but how should the value and worth of the new technology be judged? New methods are needed to evaluate the emerging benefits which are not easily quantifiable.

The decision to implement IT, the pace of IT development, and the level of IT spending is becoming increasingly a managerial judgement rather than a simple cost–benefit analysis. The IT salesman should thus be aware that managers will be seeking guidance on the success of IT usage in similar organisations as a guide to their own IT planning.

1.3 IT TRENDS

1.3.1 Changing Skills

Today's IT salesman should be aware of the changes – both scale and scope – of the uses to which information technology is now being applied. For example the evolution of the *application programming interface* has simplified the mechanical tasks involved in systems development. This has made many of the skills of programmers of the 1960s totally obsolete. Now there are new demands, the technical demands of the on-line, real-time, integrated systems and of data communications and networking.

New applications throw up new programming languages and skills affecting both user and supplier. There are new social, organisational and business demands requiring the IT supplier to help design interactive systems that are user-friendly; provide support for end-users who are either developing their own applications or using office technology services; and help find new ways to improve performance and profit. These demands are changing the nature of IT skills among the computing specialists in many organisations.

Such people will decide, or at least influence future IT purchasing strategies and the IT salesman must be equipped to understand their needs and find solutions for them.

1.3.2 Key Areas

The National Computing Centre Ltd, which exists to promote the effective use of IT, has identified and is addressing key industry trends as they are developing in the late 1980s. Familiarity with these areas will do much to enhance the credibility of the IT salesman.

End-user Computing

This is a phenomenon which originated in the early 1980s and has grown largely through the demands from end-users for their own computing facilities. Forecast trends include:

- A continuation of the data processing departments in providing *corporate* information but supplemented by the capability of end-users to process *personal* and *departmental* information.

- An increased use of IT by line managers in decision making with more sophisticated decision support systems. Since managers will require access to information held on corporate computers, external data-bases and micros, the problems of data storage, security access, transfer and reformatting will need to be addressed.

- An increased use of multifunction workstations and highly portable software packages.

- Greater efforts by IT suppliers to *interconnect* systems which conform to international standards.

- An increase in the use of publicly available services such as Value Added Network Services (VANS), public databases and conferencing systems.

Data Communications

Since it is recognised that information – the raw material for decision making – needs to be *communicated* to be effective, a sound data communications infrastructure is essential to any organisation's IT plan. Current trends include:

- lower communications costs caused by technological advance and competition in public telecommunications;
- an increase in bandwidths available;
- a proliferation of communicating microcomputers;
- improved PABX systems;
- cheaper and more popular Local Area Networks (LANs);
- the emergence of a fully Integrated Services Digital Network (ISDN);
- a variety of services, especially database and electronic mail;
- more image communication such as videotex and videoconferencing;
- integration of voice and data function in both office and factory;
- rapid growth in use by *non-technical* staff;
- growth of radio-based services which are essentially mobile, such as voice, data and fax.

Software Engineering

Software production is considered by many senior managers to be the area which offers a high potential for cost-effective computing. By the mid-1980s the expenditure required by software development and maintenance including staff costs accounted for around 69% of the cost of computing power.

The mystery which shrouded software is now disappearing through the emergence of an *engineering discipline* in its production. Software engineering is the application of an appropriate set of techniques and tools to the whole process of software production which enable a software development project team to set and meet its goals, within an acceptable cost and timescale.

Key trends in software engineering are thus:

- an increasing use of engineering disciplines (methods) will be applied to all parts of the software life cycle and will be implemented and enforced through *software tools* (Figure 1.1);

- the prime market requirement will be for well-integrated sets of software tools and the supply will be dominated by a few market leaders;

- the specifications for widely accepted methods and systems interfaces will become public domain standards;

- the most valid take-up of software engineering in development will be in the real-time community;

- a major national initiative on software quality;

- an increasing awareness of, and demand for, training;

- continuing government action, UK and European, to help establish software engineering disciplines.

Standards

The interconnection of devices and systems is an issue of mounting importance. Standards will continue to play a paramount role in enabling this to be achieved. Various levels of computer architecture will need to be standardised, including:

- networking:

  • Open Systems Interconnection (OSI),

  • Systems Network Architecture (SNA),

  • Ethernet and others;

- application-oriented protocols;

- Manufacturing Automation Protocol (MAP);

- Technical and Office Protocol (TOP);

- documentation structures and interchange;

  • X.400.

The international adoption of OSI will offer IT users freedom of choice in selecting future computing and communications devices which *inter-*

CATEGORIES OF SOFTWARE TOOLS

Source NCC STDC booklet.

Figure 1.1   Tools for Software Engineering

SOFTWARE ESTIMATING

These tools support the project management activity by assisting in the estimating of software development timescales and costs. Features include: code size estimation, using, for example, comparison with existing systems, assessment of development resources, using productivity measurement, analysis of risk, estimation of development effort, costs and timescales.

PROJECT SUPPORT ENVIRONMENTS

An integrated project support environment (IPSE) is a complete set of software engineering tools, which together provide all of the facilities necessary to execute a project with a high degree of automation of the activities involved in the life cycle. A project support environment (PSE) provides a subset of the tools provided in an IPSE. The tools may be only partially integrated. PSEs provide support for the definition and design phases, for overall technical management, and for the automatic production of documentation, source code and test data.

FOURTH GENERATION SYSTEMS

A fourth generation system (4GS) is an integrated set of software engineering tools, which has evolved to provide an environment for the support of the production and development of interactive transaction processing applications, and for ad hoc access to an applications database. Among the key characteristics of 4GS are interactive use via terminals and work-stations, with support for multi-user access, and rapid response to queries and applications processing, a data dictionary and a database; high-level end-user facilities, applications generation features possibly interfacing to COBOL or FORTRAN, free format and conversational features.

IKBS

Tools for building intelligent knowledge based systems (IKBS) are now quite common. IKBS techniques are starting to be used in the tools used for building other software systems.

PROJECT MANAGEMENT TOOLS

Project management tools are used to support the activities involved in planning projects, and the manager's need to monitoring and control actual projects, and produce reports. Typical tools allow estimating, scheduling and analysis of time and effort. They allow critical-path analysis and 'What if' analysis. Excellent reporting and charting facilities are provided, as well as financial analysis. Interactive use and multiproject use are valuable features. Fourth generation features are becoming common. Project management tools should be integrated with other tools, such as IPSEs and configuration management.

QUALITY MANAGEMENT

These assist in the management and control of product quality during software development. Quality planning and quality control are the two aspects that need to be supported. Quality planning involves planning documentation and recording, and planning distribution. Quality management involves adherence checking for project standards, for specification standards, and for coding standards. There should be support for quality milestones, quality reviews and inspections, and effectiveness measurement for V and V testing. Integration with other tools and interactive use are desirable features.

CONFIGURATION MANAGEMENT

Configuration management tools assist in the control of products generated during the development life-cycle – such as documents, code and computer media. The tools also assist in control of externally produced products, such as operating systems and software tools. The three major aspects are configuration control, software configuring, and documentation control.

ANALYSIS AND DESIGN

Specification of requirements and actual design performed before creation of actual code are the subject of the analysis and design phases of the life cycle. Tools support requirements specification and analysis, including the stages of requirements acquisition and requirements expression. Design specification and analysis are covered, including design expression, design derivation and design analysis and checking.

IMPLEMENTATION

These tools support the implementation of the final software product, starting with the lowest level (unit or module) of design specification. The code and unit test phase, the integration and final test phase, and final acceptance testing are included in implementation. There are six activities: Code production and maintenance; generation of executable code; generation of test environments; generation of software test configurations; test execution and monitoring; and test results analysis.

VERIFICATION AND VALIDATION

Verification and validation tools support specification analysis at all levels, including requirements, design and code itself. There are five activities: dynamic specification analysis; static specification analysis; source-code data analysis; correctness proving; and quality control. V & V tools have much in common with analysis and design tools and with quality management tools.

GRAPHICS TOOLS

Graphics are now an essential component of many business systems, because the cost of high-quality graphic devices has fallen so dramatically. Software developers need a whole variety of graphic tools, both for ordinary plotting and charting, and for high quality presentation graphics developments.

connect, but such users will also require the establishment of IT strategies based on the appropriate standards to ensure the compatibility of their in-house developments with their own future systems and those of their trading partners. Key trends include:

- a growing appreciation that implemented standards are necessary for the successful application of IT;

- progress in selected areas will increase the demand for action in others;

- standards making will be concerned not only with networking, applications-oriented protocols and documentation interchange, but with the validation of programming languages, operating systems, databases, and programming support environments.

It will also be important to develop standards relevant to the processes of systems analysis, design and implementation.

Expert Systems

Expert systems are being developed to solve a range of practical problems. They represent a departure from traditional methods of programming and are designed as problem-solving programs that solve substantial problems generally conceded as being difficult and requiring expertise. They are called *knowledge based* because their performance depends critically on the use of facts and heuristics used by experts (D'Agapeyeff, 1983).

The body of facts (knowledge) and the heuristics (which may be regarded as rule of thumb) are represented in the computer. The program uses the heuristics to operate on the stored knowledge in the light of a user enquiry and ideally the system's reasoning can be explained to the user to indicate how a particular conclusion was reached.

Expert systems represent a flexible approach to computer competence, drawing on specialist knowledge and exploiting various types of inference (not only deductive reasoning). An expert system is characterised by three fundamental elements:

- the knowledge manager;

- the knowledge base;

- the situation model.

The *knowledge manager* typically uses the information contained in the *knowledge base* to interpret the current contextual data in the *situation model.*

Research and development in this area may be expected to complement the mainstream fifth generation initiative.

This initiative was announced at an international conference in Tokyo in 1981 – that Japan proposed to build a *fifth-generation computer*. Previous computers had progressed through four generations: thermionic valve, transistor, integrated circuit, and Very Large Scale Integration (VLSI). The prime objective of this major initiative was to develop, by the 1990s, computers that were more powerful, more flexible and more intelligent than previously. In effect the new computers would be Knowledge Information Systems comprising high-level man–machine interfacing and the ability to solve problems.

Much information has been published on the subject through journal articles, brochures, conference proceedings and books, in particular *Towards Fifth-Generation Computers,* published by the National Computing Centre Ltd in 1983.

IT Within Manufacturing

There is growth in the use of IT within manufacturing, which involves many aspects of automation including CAD/CAM and robotics.

The International Data Corporation (IDC) estimates that the world market for industrial automation will grow from $11 billion in 1985 to $39 billion in 1990. Key trends can be summarised as follows:

- The market sectors concerned with manufacturing information systems and computerised manufacturing will grow from $5.6 billion in 1985 to $26.1 billion in 1990.

- There is continuing strong growth amongst small and medium-sized companies.

- Within larger companies already using CAD and CNC, there is an increasing interest in flexible and integrated manufacturing systems.

- The Manufacturing Automation Protocol (MAP) seems likely to become the engineering standard for communication between the various computer and control devices in an integrated system.

- The design and implementation of integrated systems will be the province of major hardware and systems suppliers and major software houses.

— Government in the UK will support the adoption of Advanced Manufacturing Technology (AMT). The EEC will also encourage the use of AMT through its 'Computers in Manufacturing (CIM) Europe' activity and the Esprit 2 programme.

Other Developments

Other trends worthy of attention of the IT salesman include:

Information Centres

The information centre is intended to reduce application backlog, cut the cost of program maintenance, and increase the availability of tools for users. It is claimed that 80% of US 'billion dollar' corporations now have information centres. Most are flexible organisations which have taken responsibility for such activities as office automation and managing personal computing.

The success of an information centre tends to be measured in terms of:

— number of new users trained;

— assistance provided;

— seminars delivered;

— equipment installed;

— information disseminated.

A shift of emphasis is seen in the second generation *knowledge* centres from administration to strategic support.

Decision Support

Decision Support Systems (DSS) are used to provide *assistance* in the decision-making process rather than to support human judgement.

Man—machine Interface

Both European and UK programs are researching human interface technology. The development of an intelligent man—machine interface will comprise:

- natural language processing;

- speech processing;

- picture and image processing.

High Availability Computers

A growing number of companies, particularly in the finance and process control application sectors are looking to *fault-tolerant* computers to fulfil their requirement for *continuous* processing. The object of such systems is to *survive* failures without loss of performance or at least to *recover* from the system failures in a degraded performance mode. The market in Europe for fault-tolerant computers was valued in 1987 at some £551 million and is growing at over 50% per annum.

SSADM

High quality systems analysis and design is an essential ingredient in every successful computer project. Inadequate analysis results in systems that do not satisfy user needs. Inadequate design produces systems that are ineffective, inefficient and inflexible. The consequences are measured in increased cost, delayed implementation, error-prone operation, and 'open-ended' maintenance.

The Structured Systems Analysis and Design Method (SSADM) offers a disciplined approach to the task within a clearly defined framework. It is now the preferred method for use by the UK Government and is spreading rapidly throughout both public and private sectors. Techniques incorporated into SSADM analysis include:

- Data Flow Diagrams (DFDs);

- Logical Data Structuring;

- Entity Life Histories.

Those used in SSADM design incorporate:

- Relational Data Analysis;

- Composite Logical Data Design;

- Process Design.

2 The Industry and the Market

2.1 IT PRODUCTS

The products and services which make up the IT industry are many and varied, being used by all manner of organisations in business, government, administrative, technical, scientific, educational and manufacturing processes.

2.1.1 Product Groups

Although complex (Tables 2.1–2.4), IT products fall into four main groups:

Hardware

Computer systems, data communications/transmission equipment and peripheral devices.

Computer hardware (the machinery) comprises mainframe systems, minicomputer and microcomputer systems. It is becoming difficult to draw dividing lines between them. However the following characteristics may help define the types currently available:

Mainframe Computers

Mainframes range from medium-sized systems to very large configurations and are particularly suited to applications giving access to very large volumes of data, where several programs need to be run at a time, or in situations requiring vast calculations. Mainframes provide economies of scale when there is a very large volume of data to be processed. They operate in two environments – multiprogramming and multiprocessing.

Group	Major classes	Other classes
Hardware Main systems	Mainframe computers	Desktop computers
	Mini/supermini computers Microcomputers – Single-user PC – Multi-user – Networking	Small-business computers Hobby/educational computers
Special systems	Distributed systems Process control systems Scientific computers CAD/CAM systems Word processing systems Laboratory systems	Attendance recording Automatic draughting Computer-aided retrieval Data collection Graphics Image processing Encoding Key to disk Viewdata Test equipment
Data communications Data transmission	Local area networks Message switching PABX Wide area networks Telex/teletex	Acoustic couplers Cables Cluster controls Concentrators Encryption devices Facsimile Fibre optics Line sharing devices Magnetic tape Modems Modem simulators Modem emulators Multiplexers Network management Protocol converters
Peripherals	Disk storage devices Displays Input devices Output devices (excluding printers) Magnetic tape drives Printers Processors (array, dedicated, front end) Readers Terminals	

Table 2.1   Hardware Products

In a *multiprogramming* environment there is one main processor. A program is executed until it is interrupted or requires an input or output (slower) operation. When this occurs, control is passed to another program. Thus only one program is being executed at a time but input or output may be going on concurrently. This provides an improved processing throughput.

In a *multiprocessing* environment there is more than one processor so that two or more programs can be executed concurrently.

Group	Major classes	Other classes
Systems software	Application program generators Programming languages File management/handling Graphics/plotting Operating systems Report generators Utilities Fourth generation systems Integrated project support environments Communications Database management Data dictionaries Network management Text processing Data entry Teleprocessing monitors	Computer performance Data integrity Information retrieval Security Videotex Viewdata Software tools (see Figure 1.1)

Table 2.2   Systems Software Products

Such processors often share the same memory and peripherals. Thus mechanisms have been devised to avoid interference with each other's data.

Minicomputers

Whereas the mainframe computer normally proceeds through a program until interrupted, the minicomputer is designed to respond to external stimuli and to take appropriate action. The mini thus tends to be *interrupt driven*. Because of this method of operation, minicomputers are particularly suited to applications which require *fast response*. Two major areas of use are in process control and screen-based systems which do not require access to large data files.

Minicomputers also play a prominent part in *distributed* systems, acting as major terminals and also front-end processors to large mainframe computers.

Microcomputers

Microcomputer systems are of two types – Personal Computer (PC) and multi-user systems. The PC (single-user) system is a stand-alone device, suitable for individuals working on their own and having little or no interaction with others. Normally they will run only one program at a time and have a limited amount of backing storage.

Multi-user microcomputers, like minicomputers, permit the central

Group	Major classes	Other classes
Applications software	Applications	Industry related*
		Profession related**
	Bespoke	
	CAD/CAM CADMAT	Computer-aided testing
		Cost estimating
		Design analysis
		Design synthesis
		Draughting
		Engineering
		Manufacturing and resource planning
		Numerical control
		Process control
	Educational	Project management
		Computer-based training
		Education and training
		Scientific
		Mathematical
	Office support	Operational research
		Local area networking
		Management support
		Office automation
		Telex/teletex
		Word processing
	Expert systems	
	Export/import	
	General purpose	
	Financial	General accounting
		Integrated accounting
		Assets accounting
		Auditing
		Cost management
		Financial planning
		HP leasing/rental
		Payroll
		Personnel records
		Pensions
		Stock control

*Industry-related applications include: Agricultural, Building societies, Banking, Construction, Property, Distribution/transport, Publishing, Estate agents, Insurance, Local Government, Public Utilities, Retailers, Wholesalers, Stockbroking, Travel agents, Tourism/hotels.

**Profession-related applications include: Architecture, Civil engineering, Legal, Market researching, Medical, Accountancy.

Table 2.3   Applications Software Products

Group	Major classes	Other classes
Computing services	Processing services Consultancy Facilities management Computer maintenance Recruitment and contract staff Training Turnkey systems Value added networking services Bespoke software Software products Combined hardware and software Database services	Accessories Ancillary equipment Arbitration Cleaning Data preparation Data transit Data interchange Electronic mail Environmental Floppy disk copying Floppy disk formatting Information databases Insurance Magnetic media supply Marketing Microfilming Media conversion Off-line printing Power supply Punched media supply Stationery Test equipment Time booking Used equipment

Table 2.4   Computing Services

processor and memory to be *shared,* so that each local user requires only a *dumb* terminal for access. However, it is also possible to use a microcomputer as a terminal with a local computing facility. Such microcomputers can be linked together to form a *network* that offers both local and shared facilities. The main shared facilities tend to be disks (storage) and printers. Central processors and memory are not shared, so that each workstation is *intelligent.*

Microcomputers can perform their more conventional functions most effectively when integrated into an *Office Automation* (OA) strategy. Such functions include: accounting, database, diary, electronic mail, graphics, spreadsheet, and word processing.

It is quite feasible to create an OA installation on microcomputers using either a multi-user system or a network complete with appropriate software. Many use icons, menus and help facilities so that the OA system is accessible to the most inexperienced IT user.

Table 2.5 shows the main data exchanges and destinations of a full-function OA system. For example, the accounting system should be capable of sending data to the database system (for reporting); to the spreadsheet system (for forecasting); and to the word processing system (for incorporation into printed reports).

Source	Accounting	Database	Electronic mail	Graphics	Spreadsheet	Word processing
Accounting	–	Yes	No	No	Yes	Yes
Database	Yes	–	No	Yes	Yes	Yes
Electronic mail	No	No	–	No	No	Yes
Graphics	No	No	No	–	No	Yes
Spreadsheet	No	Yes	No	Yes	–	Yes
Word processing	No	No	Yes	Yes	No	–

Table 2.5   Main Data Exchanges and Destinations of a Full-function OA System

Systems Software

Special programs which enable the hardware to operate efficiently; routines which carry out procedures common to virtually all installations; assemblers and language compilers which translate applications programs into machine code; and program development aids.

Among the major systems software products available are:

Operating Systems

These comprise sets of systems programs which permit the continuous operation of a computer from program to program with the minimum operator interventions. An Operating System (OS) also acts as an interface between the operator, the computer and the program being processed. An OS can be defined as (ISO, 1984):

> "Software that controls the execution of programs and that may provide services such as resource allocation, scheduling, input/output control and data management. Although OS are predominantly software, partial or complete hardware implementations are possible."

Teleprocessing Monitors

These are software packages which handle tasks such as *transaction processing* (stock enquiries, order processing, cash postings, etc) or the development of on-line application programs.

Database Management Systems (DBMS)

Since many different applications use similar files of data, systems have been developed which allow all the data to be kept in a *single* large, linked *set* of files which the different applications can use.

The maintenance of the linkages and indexes in a large database is a complex operation carried out by a piece of proprietary software – the DBMS. DBMS are produced by computer manufacturers and also a variety of software companies for use over a range of computers.

Utilities

These are programs or routines which carry out certain procedures which are common to virtually all applications and installations. They are normally provided by the computer manufacturers and written in a generalised way so that they may be used by individual users through parameters.

Utilities include:

- sorting and merging;
- housekeeping;
- file maintenance;
- security;
- file copying.

Language Assemblers and Compilers

A computer accepts instructions from an application program in machine code form which is represented in binary. Machine code is thus the lowest level of language in use. It is quite unsuitable for the programmer writing the application program. In order to overcome the difficulties in programming in machine code, it is possible to write programs, using *codes* for instructions and *labels* to reference storage locations. The means

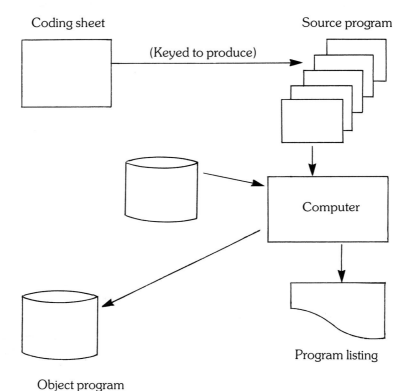

Figure 2.1   The Assembly Process

to translate them into machine code is through an *assembler* (Figure 2.1).

Although less efficient than assembly languages in terms of the employment of machine resources, the vast majority of applications programs use high-level languages, such as Cobol. It is possible to use meaningful English statements such as 'Add A to B giving C' or to express complex mathematical formulae by a single instruction.

Just as an assembly program is translated into machine code by the assembler, so the high-level language programs are converted to machine code via the *compiler*. The relationships between the various systems software entities are shown in Figure 2.2.

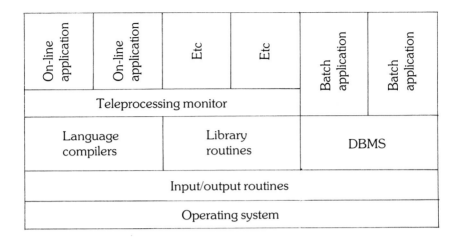

Figure 2.2   Mainframe Systems Software

Microcomputer Systems Programs

Operating Systems (OS) play a major role in today's microcomputer usage. Sometimes referred to as the executive or monitor, the OS controls the loading and execution of programs.

Other systems programs provide software tools for developing applications and are called in as required by the OS. Examples of microcomputer operating systems include:

- Control Program Monitor (CP/M) (Digital Research Inc);

- Disk Operating System (DOS) (Microsoft Inc, including PC-DOS MS-DOSI/2);

- UNIX multi-user, multitasking system (AT&T);

- PICK multi-user, multitasking system (PICK Systems Inc);

- OS2 (IBM/Microsoft Inc).

Applications Software

In addition to writing one's own application programs, the user has recourse to a vast range of applications software. These packaged programs cover a wide variety of specific functions (applications) for use in more than one environment or organisation.

Services

A wide range of specialist professional computing services is available to virtually all sectors of the IT user community. The 12 major classes of service have a major impact on the use of IT in the UK. At the time of writing the industry's trade association CSA (Computing Services Association) reported that its 275 member organisations now employed 45,793 IT specialists and in 1986/87 produced collective revenues of £1788 million.

2.1.2 Product Classes

Each product group divides into product classes as illustrated in Tables 2.1–2.4. The provision of an 'IT solution' to an organisation's needs will require a mix of products and services (Appendix 3). For example this could include:

- a minicomputer system;
- a local area network system;
- a variety of peripherals;
- a maintenance service;
- a power supply;
- a variety of systems software;
- some application packages;
- help in staff recruitment;
- specialist consultancy;
- staff training.

All and many, many more are available to any organisation, large or small, seeking IT solutions.

2.2 IT VENDORS

The industry comprises approximately 7000 (NCC *Computer Services Index,* 1988) supplier companies, the vast majority of which are very small organisations with annual turnovers of significantly less that £1 million.

There are however some major players, notably hardware systems/ telecommunications manufacturers and relatively large system/software houses, consultancies, Other Equipment Manufacturers (OEMs) and distributors.

2.2.1 Main Classes of Vendor

Computer Manufacturers

These companies design, develop, build and market mainframe, mini- and microcomputer systems. Some are involved in all three classes and include systems software, applications software and a variety of computing services in their sales portfolios. The prices of such systems range from under £500 to configurations in excess of £10 million.

It is sometimes difficult to differentiate between the three main classes of micro, mini and mainframe. Tables 2.6a–c list some 39 major manufacturers that are leaders in a variety of price ranges. Of the 39, some 13 are involved in marketing two or more classes. IBM, ICL and Unisys for example produce all three classes of computer. Many computer manufacturers sell some of their products direct to the IT user community but also through distributors, dealer networks and software houses. Some products are sold to OEMs.

Other Equipment Manufacturers

OEMs purchase hardware systems from the computer manufacturers and, having a production facility, tailor the products and provide their own software. The resultant systems are then sold to the user community.

Distributors

Distributors take products from a particular computer manufacturer or packaged software company and sell to dealers.

Dealers

Sometimes called authorised dealers or value-added retailers, these companies obtain hardware and standard software products and sell on to their 'local' market. These products are obtained either directly from the computer manufacturer or through distributors.

Some dealers specialise in a particular area of expertise and thus address

< £500	£500–£1K	£1K–£1.5K	£1.5K–£5K	£5K–£10K	£10K–£15K
Amstrad	Amstrad	IBM	IBM	IBM	LSI
Commodore	Acorn	Amstrad	Apple	ICL	IBM
Atari	Apricot	Apple	Olivetti	Unisys	Hewlett-Packard
NEC	Atari	Apricot	Compaq	Olivetti	Whitechapel
Acorn	Epson	Tandon	Apricot	NCR	Tektronics
	Spectrum	Research	Wang	Wang	Alpha Micro
		machines	Hewlett-	Data General	TDI
		Commodore	Packard	Hewlett-	Texas Instruments
		Data General	NCR	Packard	Olivetti
			Data General		Wang
					NCR
					Data General

* Source: Pedder Associates Ltd.

Table 2.6a   Leading Manufacturers of Microcomputers*

£15K–£30K	£30K–£60K	£60K–£100K
DEC	DEC	Honeywell-Bull
Hewlett-Packard	IBM	Ferranti
IBM	ICL	McDonnell-Douglas
Olivetti	Altos	ICL
Wang	Prime	IBM
Data General	Data General	Tandem
Concurrent	Norsk Data	NCR
	Concurrent	Prime
		Stratus
		Concurrent
		Data General
		Norsk Data

* Source: Pedder Associates Ltd.

**Table 2.6b   Leading Manufacturers of
Minicomputers/Super Micros***

'vertical' markets. In these cases they purchase the hardware and produce their own software product in order to provide composite systems for their particular market niche. In other cases they purchase hardware and tailor the software to meet the specific needs of a user.

£100K–£250K	£250K–£500K	£500K–£1M	> £1M
DEC	IBM	IBM	IBM
ICL	ICL	DEC	ICL
IBM	DEC	ICL	Unisys
Prime	Hewlett-Packard	Unisys	Amdahl
Stratus	Honeywell-Bull	Honeywell-Bull	Honeywell-Bull
Tandem	Unisys		NAS
NCR	NCR		CRAY
Honeywell-Bull			
Unisys			

*Source: Pedder Associates Ltd.

Table 2.6c   Leading Manufacturers of Mainframe/Super Minicomputers*

Packaged Software Companies

These organisations are originators of software products which fall under both systems and applications software categories. Like the computer manufacturers, they sell either directly or through distributors (including computer manufacturers).

Software/Systems Houses

Systems houses, which include many consultancies, provide bespoke solutions for users, sometimes in a 'turnkey' mode. Such solutions require hardware which is purchased directly from computer manufacturers or through a distributor and software which is written in house. The latter is sometimes simplified by using 'kernel software' – standard software modified to suit individual needs.

2.2.2 Professional Standards

One major problem confronting the IT industry is concerned with the standard of IT sales personnel at the lower (value) end of the market.

Chapters 3–8 of this book address the important issues of providing a sound marketing infrastructure and professional salesforce from sales trainee to sales manager. The *costs* of providing such levels of marketing and sales professionalism are *high* but justified on the grounds of meeting customer expectations. The larger IT company – whether computer manufacturer, OEM or software house – will have the financial and other

Source	Hardware and systems (£M)	Software and services (£M)	Total expenditure £M	%
Private sector purchases (based on turnover survey)	2232*	2304	4536	65
Public sector purchases (based on direct survey)	1218	1257	2475	35
Total expenditure from user analysis	3450	3561	7011	
Computer manufacturer sales (based on poll)	3600*	1500	5100	
Computer services sector sales (based on industry report)		1985	1985	
Total sales from supplier analysis	3600	3485	7085	

* Includes *c* £364 million hardware/systems sold via computer services sector.

Table 2.7   Estimated Size of the UK IT Market 1986/7

resources necessary to raise (and maintain) the professional standards of its salespeople to the levels demanded by the industry. These levels are necessary to ensure credibility, customer expectation, repeat business and growth. For the large IT supplier, selling to large organisations, this is the expected norm.

In its turn the large user organisation includes many IT experts and its information services department will have been through the 'IT buying loop' many times already. It knows what it wants, what to expect, and has the resources to pay for it.

The small organisation is not so well placed! The paradox of the IT industry is that the smaller the organisation, the less its knowledge and financial resources but the greater is its need for support. The smaller IT dealer in its turn will wish to provide maximum support but will be constrained by tight profit margins and low (competitive) selling prices. In addressing this end of the market, the IT salesman will need to operate just as professionally as his/her counterpart selling a £1 million configuration. Thus it becomes the joint responsibility of the dealer, distributor and supplier (hardware and software) to arrange joint training programmes for the salespeople. In conjunction with approved training organisations, such jointly funded programmes will do much to avoid discontent and lack of confidence among the smaller IT user community. Small they may be, but collectively they are the backbone of the UK economy.

2.3 IT MARKET

2.3.1 The Market Overall

Overview

It is useful for the IT salesman to gain an insight into the size, scope and nature of the market for IT products and services. Opinions vary as to the actual *value* of the market and it is difficult to measure accurately. However many excellent organisations – Pedder Associates, IDC UK Ltd, Quantum Science Corporation and the National Computing Centre Ltd to name but four – conduct regular surveys on the direction of IT and the buying patterns of the user community. By taking samples across all industry and product sectors, these industry watchers produce reports, analyses and forecasts of the amounts of money spent on IT and the components of that sum.

Although varying by class of industry and by size of organisation, overall spending on IT tends to break down in the following order:

	%
Hardware and systems	31
Other external costs	32
Staff costs	37

Since staff costs are generally internal they are excluded from most market sizing exercises.

Thus 63% of the overall IT budget involves the *purchase* of IT products or services, which of course comprise the portfolios of the IT salesman.

Market Size

In attempting to size the value of the UK market for IT products and services two separate approaches have been made (Table 2.7). One was based on the spending pattern of the IT user community, the other derived from a poll of the IT supplier sector. Both analyses suggested the market to be worth at least £7 billion in the year 1986/87.

Convergence Factor

The £7 billion estimate of the market is probably understated because of the blurring of traditional technology frontiers – *computing* and *communications*.

According to forecasts made by the Telecommunications Industry Research Centre (1987), the UK will have spent $3450 million (£1916 million at the 1.8 rate) on telecommunications equipment in 1987. At a conservative annual growth rate of 6% this suggests that the 1986 UK telecommunications expenditure was *c* £1600 million. It is doubtful whether this full amount was included in the survey material used in assessing the £7 billion IT expenditure – it could be closer to £8 billion!

Not long ago computing and communications were separate technologies. Today the keyword is *convergence*, which covers the provision of a *total* information service. This total service links data processing, office automation and telephony operations. Indeed a computer is at the heart of today's PABX switches, Prestel services, facsimile, telex and electronic mail technologies.

As was seen in Section 2.1, the industry we call IT includes in its product portfolios not just computer systems and services but also telephone apparatus and switchboards, mobile communications, networking equipment and services, text and graphics, CAD/CAM and process control, cable and satellite, test equipment and a variety of support services.

Convergence is not just limited to the linking of technology. Computer companies are merging or at least co-operating with communications companies, examples being ICL/STC and Olivetti/AT&T. However the widespread incorporation of computing and communications will depend greatly on the adoption of workable *standards* and *compatibility*.

One other drawback to convergence is the fact that the telephone, telex, facsimile, and data networks tend to be operated on separate or dedicated systems. On the positive side however is the introduction of digital networks such as ISDN which suits basic computer operations.

Convergence is also being reflected in company personnel structures with the emergence of the *information manager* assuming the roles of both traditional computer/DP manager and communications manager. This is the person whom the aspiring IT salesman will need to convince!

Personal Computers

Of course with the advent of the Personal Computer (PC) one could argue that the total market for IT products and services should extend to all businesses and their counterparts in the public sector. The low price of the PC with its attendant packaged software has brought IT within the financial compass of virtually the whole business community. In the UK, this business community comprises some 1.3 million organisations which are registered for value added tax. Coincidentally some 1.2 million computers were sold in 1986/7 within the UK.

In the government sector also, PC systems can be purchased by line managers without recourse to the CCTA (Central Computer and Telecommunications Agency) which concentrates its authority on all administrative systems purchased by government with a unit value of £10 thousand and above. Of course the majority of computer *units* sold have a very low unit value. Those with a value of <£500 represented 58% of the total shipped in 1986 whereas only 2% accounted for 67% of the *value* of hardware and systems sales. The overall breakdown is shown in Table 2.8.

Unit price	Sales volume		Sales value	
	Units	%	£M	%
< £500	666,000	58	121	3
£500–£15K	465,085	40	1079	30
>£15K	24,601	2	2400	67
Total	1,155,686		3600	

*Source: Pedder Associates Ltd.

Table 2.8   Breakdown of Computer Shipments in 1986

2.3.2 Growth

In 1987/8 there was an unmistakable air of optimism expressed by many industry watchers regarding the prospects for IT sales growth.

Overall Growth

The following pointers support this forecast of overall growth:

All Systems Growth (1986–1991)

According to Pedder Associates Ltd, who polled 465 IT manufacturers and vendors, the *overall* growth rate in value terms will be 16% *pa* to 1991

(Figure 2.3, Table 2.9). Growth will be especially strong in the sales of systems in the price ranges:

£15K–£30K

£30K–£60K

£250–£500K

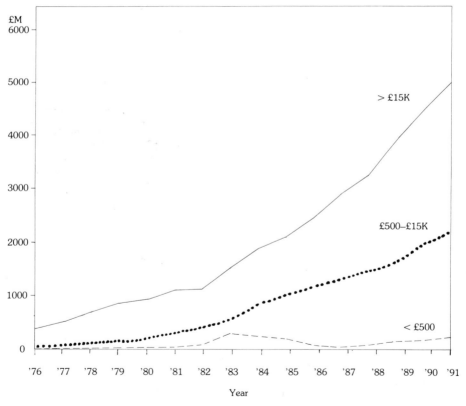

*Source: Pedder Associates Ltd.

Figure 2.3   All Systems Value Shipment Growth in the UK*

Unit price	Sales (£M) 1986	Sales (£M) 1991	Growth (%)
> £15,000	2400	5100	17
£500-£15,000	1079	2300	14
< £500			10

* Source: Pedder Associates Ltd.

Table 2.9   Forecast for Growth of all Systems*

End-user Devices Growth (1986–1991)

The *Information Technology Trends* report, published by NCC and based on a survey of user organisations, forecasts very similar growth figures in the area of end-user devices (Table 2.10). It is of particular relevance as the growth of computerisation since the early 1970s has generally meant increasing numbers of end-users coming into direct contact with their own organisation's computer system. This has occurred through the installation of terminals, microcomputers or other end-user devices in end-user departments. In most organisations data capture was the first function to be moved into the user's domain. This was rapidly followed by an on-line system incorporating data capture and on-line enquiries on corporate data.

| | Overall 5-year growth rate (%) | Individual 5-year growth rates | | |
		Lower quartile (%)	Median (%)	Upper quartile (%)
VDUs/terminals	71	25	63	112
PC-based terminals/ networked micros	365	129	285	650
Stand-alone micros	89	20	67	155
Other devices (eg POS, ATM)	130	–	75	317
All devices	109	52	90	163

*Source: NCC *Information Technology Trends*.

Table 2.10   Overall and Individual Growth of End-user Devices*

The existence of the on-line network opened up many possibilities for users to generate their own reports from corporate databases. Latterly the continued spread of the on-line networks and the availability of microcomputers have encouraged the provision of a wider range of IT facilities to end-users. They are used as tools by the end-users in many of their daily tasks – improving communications, aiding office efficiency and improving all forms of information access for control and planning – plus, the facility to develop their own personal or departmental systems.

End-user devices fall into four main categories:

– VDUs/terminals;

– linked micros, PC-based terminals, micros connected to networks;

– stand-alone micros;

– other devices (POS, ATM).

Figure 2.4 shows the number of installed end-user devices in 1986 and the forecast growth to 1991. The total number of devices is predicted to grow from 146,000 in 1986 to 305,000 in 1991 representing 109% *growth* over five years or a compound growth rate of 16% *pa.*

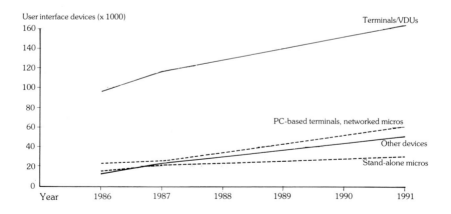

*Source: NCC *Information Technology Trends.*

**Figure 2.4   Growth in User Interface Devices 1986–1991
(Based on 686 Responses)***

Forecasts for Telecommunications Equipment Sales in US$m

1987			1990		
1.	United States	24,313.0	1.	United States	27,191.3
2.	Russia	9,800.0	2.	Russia	13,402.0
3.	Japan	7,100.0	3.	Japan	8,456.0
4.	West Germany	6,100.0	4.	West Germany	7,684.0
5.	France	4,960.0	5.	Italy	6,734.0
6.	Italy	4,522.0	6.	France	6,161.0
7.	United Kingdom	3,450.0	7.	United Kingdom	4,718.0
8.	Canada	1,927.0	8.	Spain	3,000.0
9.	China	1,752.0	9.	Canada	2,321.0
10.	Spain	1,650.0	10.	India	2,282.0
11.	South Korea	1,494.0	11.	China	2,050.0
12.	India	1,462.0	12.	South Korea	1,919.0
13.	Australia	1,360.0	13.	Australia	1,732.0
14.	Switzerland	1,150.0	14.	South Africa	1,511.0
15.	South Africa	1,142.0	15.	Switzerland	1,393.0
16.	Sweden	966.0	16.	Mexico	1,307.0
17.	Mexico	946.0	17.	Sweden	1,144.0
18.	Brazil	895.0	18.	Austria	1,080.0
19.	Austria	805.0	19.	Brazil	1,024.0
20.	Indonesia	704.0	20.	Taiwan	913.0
21.	Taiwan	698.0	21.	Indonesia	875.7
22.	Argentina	697.0	22.	Netherlands	786.5
23.	Saudi Arabia	611.0	23.	Argentina	772.0
24.	Hong Kong	609.0	24.	Saudi Arabia	770.2
25.	Netherlands	562.0	25.	Hong Kong	705.4
26.	Norway	518.0	26.	Norway	643.0
27.	East Germany	464.0	27.	East Germany	601.9
28.	Belgium	436.0	28.	Pakistan	539.6
29.	Venezuela	428.0	29.	Belgium	519.0
30.	Greece	339.0	30.	Greece	502.9
31.	Pakistan	328.0	31.	Venezuela	481.9
32.	Singapore	328.0	32.	Singapore	427.7
33.	Finland	314.0	33.	Turkey	402.8
34.	Denmark	295.0	34.	Denmark	370.4
35.	Turkey	294.0	35.	New Zealand	367.5
36.	New Zealand	257.0	36.	Finland	363.6
37.	Bangladesh	246.0	37.	Bangladesh	317.3
38.	Poland	231.0	38.	Poland	304.9
39.	Egypt	228.0	39.	Iraq	283.0
40.	Hungary	211.0	40.	Egypt	280.0
41.	Iraq	201.0	41.	Czechoslovakia	273.9
42.	Yugoslavia	188.0	42.	Hungary	252.3

* Source: Telecommunications Industry Research Centre forecasts.

Table 2.11   World's Top 42 Markets (Reproduced from the
***Financial Times*, 19 October 1987)**

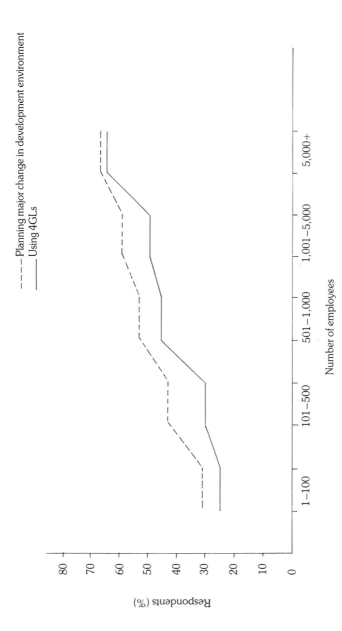

*Source: NCC *Information Technology Trends.*

Figure 2.5   Incidence of 4GLs, Program Generators or Prototypers*

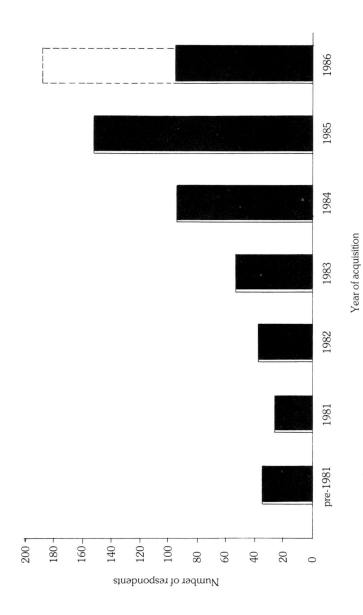

*Source: NCC *Information Technology Trends.*

Figure 2.6 Year in which 4GLs, Program Generators or Prototypers were Obtained*

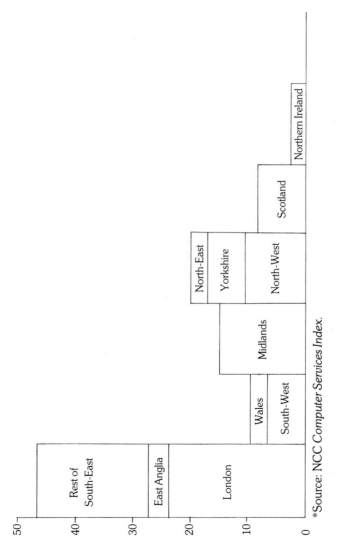

*Source: NCC Computer Services Index.

Figure 2.7　Percentage Distribution (Geographical) of 8,570 Major Computer Users*

Telecommunications Growth (1987–1990)

According to TIRC (Telecommunications Industry Research Centre) forecasts, the UK will remain in seventh position in the world's top 50 markets for telecommunications equipment sales with annual growth rates exceeding 8% (Table 2.11). Intense competition and massive structural changes with a proliferation of corporate alliances, joint ventures, mergers and takeovers make this sector of IT possibly the most exciting of all!

Software Tools Growth

The use of program generators, prototypers or Fourth Generation Languages (4GLs) is spreading rapidly in data processing departments (Figure 2.5). The range is wide but most of these software products are viewed as tools for IT professionals to use in reducing project development times or creating applications prototypes. Some products are specialised report generators or query program generators whilst others are comprehensive application development systems.

NCC's *Information Technology Trends* concludes that almost all of the products cited had been acquired relatively recently (Figure 2.6). Clearly the use of such products has grown significantly since 1984 and a poll of users indicates that over 50% of the respondents were convinced that major changes in their IT environments would occur by 1988/89. The vast majority suggested that the acquisition and use of a 4GL or the extension of an existing 4GL was the planned direction of change.

A further spur to the growth potential of 4GL sales is the number of organisations *changing* their hardware systems and using the 4GL in the conversion process.

2.3.3 Market Sectors

Overview

Geographically some 46% of computers installed are in the London/South-East area (Figure 2.7).

The total market for IT products and services comprises three segments:

- — UK public sector;
- — UK private sector;
- — international sector.

Assessing the size and potential of the world market for IT products is beyond the scope of this book, therefore the remainder of Chapter 2 will concentrate on the UK market. However the following should be borne in mind:

– All or most of the uses to which IT is put in the UK are equally applied in Europe, the Middle East, South-East Asia, Japan, Australasia and of course the USA and Canada.

– Thus the market is truly *international*.

– Many hardware and software products are dominated by US companies, nursed to this condition by sheer size and scope of that market.

– Such a growth market always allows new entrants, especially where there is a reputation for IT skills. The UK has this reputation especially in the software sector.

– The UK shares a common language with the USA which gives it an edge over many foreign competitors.

Public Sector

The public sector market for IT divides as follows:

Central Government

This comprises some 600 departments and sub-departments, including the major ministries/departments for:

– Customs and Excise;

– Defence;

– Education and Science;

– Employment;

– Energy;

– Environment and Transport;

– Foreign and Commonwealth Affairs;

– Health and Social Security;

– Home Affairs;

- Inland Revenue;

- National Savings;

- Trade and Industry;

- Finance (Treasury).

Central government employs some 18,500 departmental staff in administrative IT, including approximately 10,000 (executive officer grade and above) with functional IT specialisation. Total IT expenditure in 1986/87 was of the order of £1.6 billion, approximately 1% of total public expenditure. Within HM Treasury, the Central Computer and Telecommunications Agency (CCTA) is responsible for advising and supporting government departments and a limited number of non-departmental public bodies in the identification and assessment of IT applications and in the selection of systems and equipment. Thus the CCTA is the major authority concerning the procurement of IT products in the administration of central government. The CCTA suggests that there will be an increasing penetration of IT systems in support of the business aims and objectives of departments.

A significant indicator of growth is the CCTA's prediction of the use of terminals in departments:

1987	65,000
1992	155,000
1995	240,000
1999	350,000

Local Government

This sector, vastly experienced in IT from the days of unit accounting machines and punched cards to present computer systems, now comprises 510 local authorities which are divided as shown in Table 2.12. The current external IT expenditure is probably in excess of £400 million, based on the following data:

- Total employees: 2,585,805

- Estimated spending level per employee: £247*

*NCC *Information Technology Trends.*

	England	Wales	Scotland	N Ireland	Total
Metropolitan districts	36				36
Non-metropolitan districts	296	37	53	26	412
Metropolitan counties	6				6
Non-metropolitan counties	39	8			47
Regional councils			9		9
Total	377	45	62	26	510

Table 2.12   Division of Local Authorities Within the UK

— Estimated breakdown of IT budget*:

    Hardware   31%

    Other external 32%

    Staff   37%

— Estimated total IT expenditure by the sector:

$$\frac{2,585,805 \times 247 \times 63}{100} = £401 \text{ million}$$

Public Utilities

Although British Gas has been privatised and now operates as a public limited company, it has characteristics similar to the other public utilities and is therefore included in this segment. Therefore the three major 'public' utilities are gas, water and electricity. All operate throughout the UK, with further divisions such as:

— Electricity Council (England and Wales):

    ● generating board (CEGB),

    ● distribution boards;

— North of Scotland Hydro Electric Board:

*NCC *Information Technology Trends.*

- generation and distribution;
- South of Scotland Electricity Board:
  - generation and distribution;
- Water Authorities Association:
  - water authorities;
- Water Companies Association:
  - water companies.

Like local authorities they are major employers, current establishment strengths being of the order:

Gas	86,096
Electricity	146,861
Water c	70,000
Total c	302,957

The external IT expenditure is probably of the order of £160 million, based on:

- total employees: 302,958
- estimated IT spending levels per employee: £823*
- estimated breakdown of IT budget*:

Hardware	33%
Other external	30%
Staff	37%

- Estimated total IT expenditure by the sector:

$$\frac{302{,}958 \times 823 \times 63}{100} = £157 \text{ million}$$

*NCC *Information Technology Trends.*

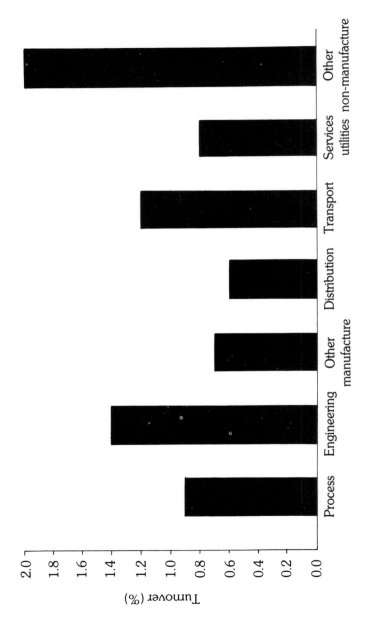

* Source: NCC *Information Technology Trends.*

Figure 2.8   Median Estimated Annual DP/IT Spending as a
Proportion of Turnover by Industry Sector

Since the annual revenues of the three utilities account for more than £2 billion and the average external IT expenditure for the utilities sector is around 0.8% of turnover, the estimate is probably reasonable.

National Health Service

The NHS, which is a major user of IT, comprises 14 regional health authorities, which control the 191 district health authorities and hospitals. The current IT expenditure is of the order of £200 million.

Private Sector

The total number of organisations registered for VAT in 1986 was 1,292,431. Of these approximately 10% have turnovers in excess of £500,000 and can be regarded as the main private sector market. By turnover the market divides as shown in Table 2.13. The level of IT spending varies between industries as does the breakdown of expenditure between hardware costs, software and other external costs, and internal staff costs. Both are illustrated in Figure 2.8 and Table 2.14.

Type of organisation	Turnover (x £1000)					
	501–1,000	1,001–2,000	2,001–5,000	5,001–10,000	> 10,000	Total
Sole proprietors	4,680	1,738				6,418
Partnerships	8,736	4,445				13,181
Companies	44,808	28,157	20,953	7,923	9,376	111,217
Total	58,224	34,340	20,953	7,923	9,376	130,816

Table 2.13   Division of UK Private Sector Market

Within the broad industry classification are a whole range of vertical markets, ranging from estate agents to motor dealers, travel agencies to professional accountants and insurance brokers to solicitors. Each group has very similar IT needs and many suppliers specialise in particular sectors.

	Hardware costs (%)	Staff costs (%)	Other costs (%)
Broad Industry Category			
Process	28	38	34
Engineering	34	34	32
Other manufacture	27	41	32
Distribution	37	35	28
Transport	22	38	41
Finance	30	36	34
Local government	31	38	32
Education/research	39	34	26
Services/utilities	33	37	30
Other non-manufacture	32	36	32
Computing	25	61	14
Other sectors	25	51	24
Organisation Size			
1–100	25	42	33
101–500	31	36	32
501–1000	30	35	35
1001–5000	29	41	30
5000+	31	35	34
Total Sample	31	37	32

* Source: NCC *Information Technology Trends.*

Table 2.14   Breakdown of DP/IT Budget

3 IT Marketing

The marketing function is arguably the most important in today's IT company. Its activities identify the very nature of the business itself and its future direction. The IT salesman is a link – the final link in the marketing chain whether he/she is located at a branch or at headquarters with responsibility for a major account.

It is important that the salesman should understand fully the role that marketing plays in the ultimate success and future of the company and his/her responsibilities within marketing. Not only does marketing provide the salesman with a vital support service but it also offers a management career path through its many and varied activities (Figure 3.1).

3.1 THE MARKETING ENVIRONMENT

Before considering the marketing process it is important to appreciate that all companies operate in a *dynamic environment* over which they have no control. This can inhibit accurate planning, especially in the long term. Thus all marketing activities must take account of changes in and features of the environment, examples including:

Economic Environment

- Economic growth:
  - per capita income,
  - distribution of wealth;
- government policy:
  - taxation,

- interest rates,
- investment subsidies.

Political Environment

- Party policy:
  - wage controls,
  - attitude to imports,
  - attitude to foreign investment,
  - attitude to trade unions.

Legal Environment

- Legislation:
  - patents,
  - trade marks,
  - Sale of Goods Act,
  - consumer credit.

Socio-cultural Environment

- Population size, growth, age distribution;
- education levels;
- literacy;
- occupational, consumption patterns.

Technological Environment

- Inventions;
- change;
- international industry standards.

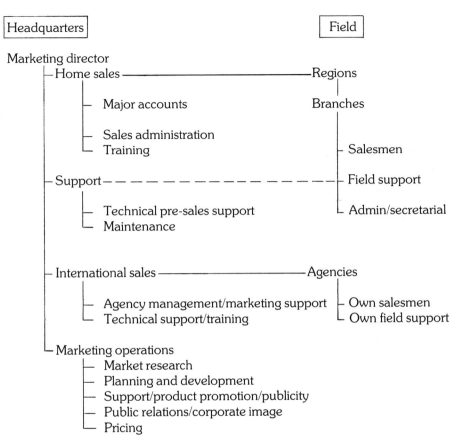

Figure 3.1   Marketing Organisation

3.2 THE MARKETING CONCEPT

Marketing is often perceived as another name for *selling*, with the functions of advertising and public relations added for good measure. Not true! Marketing in its true sense is *the management process responsible for identifying, anticipating and satisfying customer requirements profitably*, whereas *selling* is the final but essential stage of the marketing process.

Thus from the salesman's viewpoint, marketing provides him/her with:

- the right product;

- at the right time;

- at the right price;

- all the supporting forces needed to maximise the chances of making sales.

3.3 THE MARKETING PROCESS

The activities necessary for an IT company to identify opportunities and cause the development of products to meet these opportunities comprise:

- market research;

- market analysis;

- market quantification;

- market strategies;

- new product considerations;

- product life cycle.·

However the marketing process is also concerned with:

- buyer behaviour;

- selling strategies.

It is useful to examine the process in further depth.

3.4 MARKET RESEARCH

Although sometimes maligned, market research can be used effectively to identify marketing opportunities and assemble information necessary to control or adjust the *marketing mix* (see Section 3.7.1). It can be undertaken as a one-off exercise or as a continuous monitoring process, using one's own staff or commissioning specialists. Methods employed include:

- Desk research

Much general market data can be gleaned from published sources such as reference and year books, directories, catalogues, Yellow Pages, government statistics, newspapers, technical journals, and subscriber services. Cuttings services can be most valuable.

— Original research

This is necessary when information is required on customer attitudes, new product design requirements or pricing exercises.

Often this can be achieved by sampling, using salesmen or the customers themselves.

Unless it is being used to uncover facts, market research should only be employed to test hypotheses.

Much literature on the subject is available and for further advice the Institute of Marketing is recommended.

3.5 MARKET ANALYSIS

3.5.1 Segmentation

All IT companies require an accurate view of the potential customer base. This is achieved through a process of market segmentation, through which the market can be analysed into groups of similar prospects, with similar characteristics and similar requirements. The resultant classification of *types* of prospects will not only help define those groups with a high sales potential but will also point to ways in which higher sales volumes within such groups can be achieved.

3.5.2 Segmentation Criteria

The ways in which the market can be segmented for analysis and planning purposes are many and varied. In practice, however, only a few criteria, possibly different for each product, will provide any particular insights.

The following are examples of typical segmentation criteria which may be combined to form a two or more dimensioned matrix:

Size of Prospect

— Arbitrary breaks in turnover, say, £1−5 million
                                                £5−10 million
                                                £10−50 million

£50–100 million
> £100 million

 — number of employees, say, <500
           500–1,000
           1,000–5,000
           >5,000

Geographical

 — Countries;

 — arbitrary lines on maps (counties).

Industry

 — Major segments:

  • government,

  • finance,

  • distribution,

  • construction,

  • retail;

 — finer segments:

  • central government,

  • local government,

  • public utilities,

  • higher education.

Hardware

 — Major manufacturers (using):

  • DEC,

  • IBM,

  • ICL,

- Honeywell-Bull,
- Unisys,
- NCR,
- Olivetti,
- Prime,
- Tandem.

Languages

- Main languages used:
    - Cobol,
    - PL/1,
    - RPG3,
    - Pascal,
    - Basic.

3.6 MARKET QUANTIFICATION

3.6.1 Sales Forecasting

Most IT companies will produce a corporate plan to cover at least a five-year period. An integral part of the corporate plan is a realistic set of sales forecasts. Whilst short-term forecasts can derive from an analysis of prospect lists, the task of forecasting for three to five years ahead can stretch uncertainty to the limit – especially if a new and unproven product is in the equation.

3.6.2 Stages

Sales forecasting goes through three major stages.

Market Potential

This is an attempt to determine by unit volume and/or value the total size of the market – assuming that every organisation which could justify a purchase did so. It thus assumes that if there is a problem, the prospect is aware of it; that he knows the product available to solve the problem; and that he purchases the product immediately. Often undertaken segment by segment, this stage indicates an *upper band* for sales of each *type* of product by *all* suppliers. This potential can increase proportionately to the population of buyers over time.

The market potential of many IT products is dependent upon the sales of a particular type of computer. Thus the sales forecaster requires access to specialist databases in order to determine the total potential for a product.

Market Demand

This is a forecast of the success that *all* suppliers to the market *might* have in total. In other words – *total market penetration*.

It can be difficult to obtain accurate data on current or past demand. Specialist market researchers can however secure sales data from specific companies and produce forecasts based on these samples. From these estimates a forecast of the future market demand, say 3–5 years, can be made, albeit tempered by the upper limit of market potential. Market demand is generally considered in the context of potential *new* business.

Market Share

Most IT companies will aim to secure a certain share of the market demand. In most IT product fields a share in excess of 10% might take some explaining, such is the level of competition. The narrower and more specific the definition of the target market, the more defensible becomes the higher market share objective. Resultant sales targets will take into account:

- a share of new business;

- add-on business from existing customers;

- wins from the competition (which do not affect the aggregate market penetration).

Sales Target Review

Having reached a position whereby numbers can be placed on possible sales, and priorities established concerning those market segments offering the higher potential, the sales operation can be planned and costed.

Should insufficient profit seem forthcoming, a review can be undertaken to consider the effects of:

— adding market segments;

— removing market segments;

— tuning the marketing programme;

— modifying the sales targets.

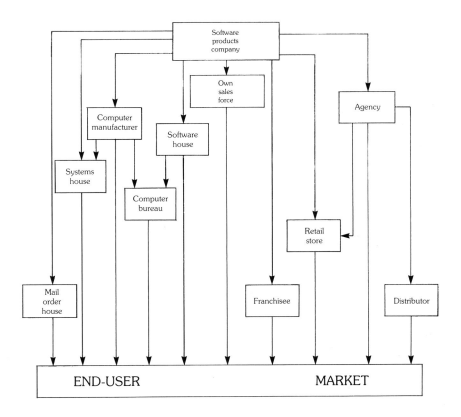

Figure 3.2   Software Products Distribution Channels

3.7 MARKETING STRATEGIES

3.7.1 The Marketing Mix

As stressed earlier, in the final analysis the success or otherwise of an IT product in the marketplace will rest on the salesman. All other marketing functions aim to ensure that the salesman has the right product, at the right time and all the support he/she needs to obtain sales. The strategies and activities are called collectively the marketing mix – the product and sales support functions designed to give the salesman all he/she needs.

As the company grows and sales increase, the requirements and responsibilities of the marketing functions will be undertaken by dedicated staff. It should be understood that in many IT companies, the costs of marketing, including sales costs, can amount to over 50% of the product sales income. Excluding direct sales costs – salaries, bonus payments, commission and expenses – the remaining marketing costs can range from between 10% and 15% of sales revenues to as much as 30%–40% for some products.

3.7.2 Distribution Channels

Figure 3.2 shows the various ways by which software can reach today's market. No single route is exclusively the best, and different segments of the market will utilise different channels.

Using Distributors and Agents

The use of distributors and agents is of particular relevance to IT companies wishing to establish a presence overseas. The difference between distributors and agents is as follows:

Distributor

A distributor is licensed to sell products *direct* to end-users and is responsible for providing support services and first-line maintenance. Examples include not only other software houses but systems houses and even mail order 'publishing' houses for low-priced micro software products.

Agent

An agency is licensed to market a product *exclusively* in one or more countries. The agency may be a distributor also, but has the power to appoint distributors in his/her territory. An agency is the distributors' local point for second-line maintenance and support and the channel for all marketing and technical communication with the UK supplier.

There is much to commend using an agency to set up a distribution network in a 'new' country since the tasks of selecting, managing and controlling distribution in that country are effectively delegated. In Japan an agency is virtually mandatory.

Selecting Agents

The disadvantage of using an agent is apparent when sales performance falls below par. Thus the selection of an agency becomes a major marketing issue and involves:

Identification

Sources of information on possible agents include:

- reference books:

  - *International Software Year Book,*

  - *Computing Services Association,*

  - *European CSA,*

  - *ICP Directory;*

- government:

  - DTI,

  - BOTB;

- embassies:

  - trade attachés in embassies (UK and overseas countries).

Qualification

Potential agents should satisfy the evaluation criteria shown in Table 3.1.

Suitability

Experience in selling IT products?
Experience in selling similar IT products?
Size? (Too large to take us seriously? Too small to be able to meet
  our sales targets?)
Ability to sell?
Ability to support sales?
Ability to provide first-line maintenance?
Feedback from existing customers?
Assessment of key staff?

Commitment

Up-front financial payment?
Agreement to minimum sales targets?
Money put aside for product launch?
Number of staff to be trained? (Who is paying?)
Allocation of resources to launch?
Are key managers committed?

Financial

Ownership?
Financial rating?
Analysis of profit and loss and balance sheets?
Adequate funding for future growth?
Acceptance terms negotiated?

Table 3.1   Evaluation Criteria for Distributors and Agents

Negotiation

Following satisfactory negotiation a formal licence agreement will be
signed by both parties (Table 3.2). Note that it is usual for the contract to
be general, with definitions of the products, territories, pricing and other
variables contained in appendices.

Pre-amble	Date of agreement, parties to agreement, etc
Definitions	To clarify any particular terms used, such as 'licensed products', 'licensed territories', 'commission'
Licence	Grant of licence over territory, product area, etc. Defines boundaries, exclusivity or otherwise, and any other conditions
Territory	Defines territory (normally geographic) in which sales are allowed
Term	Defines length of agreement, renewal and notice conditions
Pricing	Defines pricing conditions and constraints on licensee
Compensation	Defines what, how, and when licensee is to pay licensor for sales made
Delivery	Defines conditions under which product is deemed to have been made available to licensee. Target sales conditions usually start after delivery
Contract	Defines minimum terms under which licensee can sub-licence to its customers, in order to protect licensor
Responsibilities	Often three sections which define responsibilities of licensee (to sell, maintain, reach certain minimum targets); licensor (to update product, fix bugs in a timely manner, etc); and mutual (work together to determine future facilities etc)
Property	Defines licence to copyrights, trademarks, patents, to allow licensee to sell, without taking away licensor's rights
Confidentiality	Defines obligations on both parties to maintain this
Termination	Defines terms and conditions which will apply in various forms of contract termination, whether for cause (one side or the other is in serious breach of contract, for non-performance or bankruptcy) or notice, or mutual agreement
Warranty	Licensor warrants the product is his, works, and that nothing else is outstanding (such as litigation) which could affect licence
Limitation of Liability	Limits claims allowable by either party
Force majeure	Limits claims due to unforeseen circumstances such as war
Notices	Describes formal channels of communication
Waiver	Defines whether, say, one unreported breach does not invalidate contract
Whole agreement	States this contract supercedes all others
Applicable law	Defines which countries' laws are to operate

Table 3.2   Typical Distributor Licence Terms

	Essential	Desirable
Agent training and maintenance		
Sales training aids		★
Support training aids		★
Technical specification	★	
Source coding		★
Wholesale price list or discount structure	★	
Bug reporting system	★	
User feedback system		★
Sales Material		
Sample documentation		
– brochures, proposal inserts, mailers		★
– concepts and facilities manual	★	
– reference cards		★
User, programmer, installation manuals	★	
Proforma customer contract		★
Demonstrations, presentations		★
Sample advertisements		★
Case histories, reference sites		★
Sales hints (objection handling, qualification checklist)		★
Other items (for distributor/agent)		
Pricing and discount structure	★	
Agency licence agreement	★	
Distributor to supplier reporting procedures	★	
Distributor to supplier payment procedures	★	
Other items (supplier)		
Change/new feature evaluation procedures	★	
Development change control procedures	★	
Distributor performance evaluation	★	
Financial protection (eg exchange control)	★	
Export documentation etc	★	

**Table 3.3   Checklist of Product and Sales Aids for
Distributors and Agents**

Equipping Agents and Distributors

A distributor will wish to provide his/her salesforce with similar levels of support as is given to the supplier's own salesteam. Thus the enlightened IT supplier using this distribution channel will provide the necessary training and product and sales aids as suggested in Table 3.3.

Managing Agents and Distributors

A continuous flow of information both ways is an integral part of agency management, including:

Sales Reports

These should include period reports of sales achieved with quarterly and yearly forecasts.

Technical Exchange

These comprise usage hints and maintenance. In the case of software products the latter will include a bug reporting and error system.

Marketing Data

Examples are sales tips, reference calls, examples of packaging and documentation, and market feedback for evaluation and subsequent product enhancement.

Finance

Financial reports including all transfer of funds.

Apart from possibly bug (software fault) reporting and fixing (fault correction), all communications should be delegated to one person in each of the companies, probably at product manager level.

Licences and Contracts

Frequently, the user of an IT product, such as software, is not entitled to the copyright of the code in which it is written. The user is normally granted a licence to use the product either indefinitely (perpetual licence) or for a finite period (lease or rental). The agent or distributor will normally complete its own product licence (Table 3.4) having first agreed terms with the supplier (Table 3.2).

Pre-amble	Date of agreement, parties to agreement, etc
Licence	Grant of licence for product(s) – usually defined completely on an attachment – and use (non-exclusive, location, period, etc)
Obligations	What the selling company will do in terms of installation, education, and maintenance. Again details may be contained on an attachment
Payment	Payment conditions (eg monthly in advance). Treatment of taxes such as VAT etc
Ownership	Customer given right to *use* product, but ownership still rests with supplier
Assignment	Customer not normally allowed to assign product elsewhere. Not normally allowed to use elsewhere than at designated location
Termination	Conditions and actions should licence be terminated by either side
Warranty	Warrants that the product works according to relevant reference manual
Limitation of liabilities	Limits amount and conditions for which supplier will accept responsibility. In particular will limit consequential losses
Legal terms	For example: waiver, notices, applicable law, whole agreement, recovery of legal costs

Table 3.4   Typical Product Licence Terms

3.7.3 Packaging and Support

Product Packaging

Most IT companies develop a *theme* which projects the company, product line or individual product. The theme is expressed through *logos* and *colours* and should be continued through all the packaging, sales aids, advertising and promotional material. For example, a tape reel and its box or a floppy disk and its sleeve should be designed to reflect the theme.

Similarly ring binders for product manuals should include the theme on both the cover and spine.

Brochures, data sheets and other promotional material will use typeset copy and colour printing. The design, setting and printing of promotional material and the production of copy is a highly skilled business. Such people are to be found in the creative departments in advertising companies, but some IT companies produce the work in house, using the services of a local printer.

Marketing managers will take account of the following in packaging their products:

— Maintain a *single,* consistent theme — logo, product name, etc — throughout *all* documentation.

— Ensure that the theme is *striking.*

— Full colour is expensive, but often the use of a *single* bold colour can achieve almost as much to highlight the message.

— Break down the cost of print production into basic elements and ensure that each item is being used effectively. For example, a theme can be built around a single base document — possibly coloured — and *overprinted* for a variety of purposes.

— Plan print runs to minimise items such as *wash up* charges when changing colour, and avoid the use of expensive stationery on long runs.

— Although typeset always looks better than typewritten copy, consider the scope for enhancing word processor documents by the use of Letraset headings, careful choice of typeface, and size and use of full, proportional spacing. For user manuals there is little wrong with good word processing. For single-page sales leaflets the cost of typeset copy is usually worthwhile.

— Ensure the product documentation is comprehensive but *easy* to understand. This alone can reduce the need for considerable vast-sales support in explaining what the product is and how to use it.

— Expurgate technical jargon.

Support

In addition to product documentation, support includes the presence of technical staff at sales branches. Such consultants operate in a pre- and post-sales capacity, answering technical questions and undertaking installation work. Further support for the end-user often includes:

- a central help desk or hot-line facility;

- the encouragement of user groups;

- a quarterly company or product newsletter;

- a product update mail-out to all customers.

3.7.4 Advertising and Promotion

Purpose

The purpose of this major marketing function is to:

- educate the market;

- project the company image;

- project the product image;

- stimulate sales enquiries;

- confirm to users the wisdom of their choice.

Many IT companies commission external marketing consultants or advertising agencies where many of the best creative skills are located.

Techniques

These include:

- display advertising;

- mail-shots;

- press releases;

- editorial coverage.

Media

The vehicles for advertising and promotion include:

- national and trade papers;

- magazines;

- TV and radio;

- published directories, including Prestel.

Usage Criteria

The questions of whether to advertise at all, how much to rely on advertising and the mix of advertising and other promotional spending will depend on the product and the market segment being addressed. For example, if the market so identified is all UK clearing banks, then the segment may be better reached *directly* using mail-shots or direct telephone selling. In this case there would be little benefit in using advertising to attract enquiries. However there could be a major benefit to the IT company wishing to project an *image* of a 'sizeable and well-established supplier' through advertising in the national press.

The costs of advertising and promotion are carefully considered before mounting major projects. Excluding the cost of product launches, which can exceed £100,000 for press coverage, press shows, seminars and demonstration, advertising and promotion can still account for 5%–7% of anticipated sales revenue. Thus when finance for a new product is authorised, provision for each promotion should be made *at the time*. It can become difficult to raise such funds subsequently.

Choosing an advertising agency is very much like choosing a distributor and the marketing manager will take similar steps. In discussions with the agency, the marketing manager will emphasise both the objective of the promotion and the probable size of the budget in which to work.

At the conclusion of a campaign or at the year end, the effectiveness of promotion should be measured against the budget. Advertisements and mail-shots should invite responses. Not only should these responses be counted but also *followed up,* in order to determine how many become qualified prospects and then customers.

Other Promotional Work

Other promotional activities include:

- attendance at exhibitions and trade shows;

— seminars;

— courses.

3.7.5 Pricing

Parties to Pricing

Pricing of products is normally related to profit, and decisions are often taken, or at least ratified, by senior management. In addition to marketing management, other parties are involved in the exercise, notably the accountant, whose aim is to help management take pricing decisions by providing data on anticipated product costs.

Depending on the organisation, a further participant could be the product manager who has ultimate responsibility for the financial margins achieved by the product and its contribution to corporate revenues. If the company's organisation is a matrix, combining both functional activities and product decentralisation, then the product manager will be a key player in the pricing game.

Influences

Generally price is influenced by cost and what the market will bear (perceived cost). However other factors can influence the price of a product and are related to specific company objectives or to competitive activity. Should the (normal) objective be to maximise profit from the product, then the cost information will help management determine the price at which profits *appear* to be maximised. Should the objective be to maintain employment in a part of the organisation then the price might be pitched lower to keep the plant operative. In a competitive market such as IT, the prices charged by other companies vying for the same business will certainly influence the pricing decision.

Pricing Strategies

A variety of pricing strategies are available to the marketing team. They include:

Market Penetration Strategy

By pricing *low,* higher sales volumes are encouraged and a larger market share is secured. Low prices tend to discourage the competition but the Return On Investment (ROI), especially of product development costs, takes longer to materialise. This strategy thus aims to maximise *long-term* profit.

Market Skimming Strategy

By pricing *high* initially, the company can extract a premium from those prospective customers known to place a high value on possessing the product. Over a period of time the price is lowered in order to trawl the next layer of prospects. Thus market skimming aims to maximise *short-term* profits by reaching top customers and then exploiting the rest of the market gradually. The strategy is of particular importance when the product is new and *unique* and when it would take time for the competition to match it.

Perceived Pricing Strategy

This can be defined loosely as what the company perceives the market is prepared to pay. It may be pursued when the company or its product has a very *high quality image,* placing it in a class higher than the competition. Discounts might be offered to a difficult prospect but this option requires the endorsement of the marketing manager.

Full Cost Strategy

This method involves firstly the calculation of the *total cost* of producing a fixed number of units. The elements comprise the manufacturing (factory) costs, a true allocation of factory, administration and selling overheads, and an agreed mark up (profit margin). The total of these elements divided by the number of units produced, becomes the full cost unit price of the product. The method has the advantage of providing management with an accurate assessment of the true cost of the product, which if sold in appropriate numbers will guarantee the required profit margin. If other, competitive companies use the same method it also encourages price stability.

The problem with this method occurs should the market not accept the final price. In this event, the required sales volumes will not be realised, the fixed costs will not be recovered and the profit becomes a loss. However, the method is suited to the pricing of a new and different product without as yet any competition or established market price for comparison. Of course as competitive products intrude over a period of time the selling price may have to be reduced to maintain sales volumes.

Rate of Return Strategy

An important indicator of company efficiency is the rate of return it achieves on capital employed. Capital includes both investment and working capital. Although the full cost price method might guarantee an adequate mark up on the total costs of the product, its return on capital employed may be unacceptable. In such a case the unit selling price of the product would need to be raised to produce an acceptable rate of return. The revised mark up on cost, expressed as a percentage, would be a function of the equation:

$$\frac{\text{Capital employed}}{\text{Annual cost}} \times \text{Required rate of return } (\%) = \% \text{ Mark up on cost}$$

This *rate of return* pricing method is of particular value when choosing future products. One product might, on the basis of full costing, offer a sound mark up on total costs but, because of its capital requirements, fail to produce a satisfactory return on investment. Like the full price method, it ignores elasticity of demand and the effect of competition on market prices. However it is similarly relevant when the product is new to the market and different from all others.

Marginal Cost Strategy

Marginal cost pricing is much more flexible than either the total cost or rate of return methods. Both the latter methods ignore the premise that once the fixed costs have been recovered by normal production, only the *variable* costs, proportional to production remain. Thus it is possible to *reduce* an otherwise artificially high selling price and possibly increase sales volumes.

If the plant is operating below capacity, marginal cost pricing could be applied and additional sales made without affecting the fixed costs. Marginal cost pricing does however require caution. A sudden reduction in price would not please a customer who had purchased the product earlier and any suggestion of price instability could result in a loss of customer confidence.

3.7.6 Selling Strategies

In Chapters 4 through 8 we shall explore in some depth the role of IT salespeople; how they become professionals; how they are selected, trained and supported; and how they might approach the job.

In concluding this section on the marketing strategies undertaken to support the salespeople, mention should be made of the selling strategies which are an essential ingredient of the marketing mix. They include:

- determining the type of salespeople required to represent the company;

- assessing the levels of support needed by the salesforce;

- motivating and leading them to success;

- allocating fair and manageable territories;

- guiding them in planning sales activities with optimum coverage;

- disseminating market intelligence;

- fighting their battles.

3.8 PRODUCT LIFE CYCLE

3.8.1 Introduction, Growth and Decline

No product lasts forever but the marketing process is continuous. Thus marketing is much concerned with the *product life cycle,* which in the IT business can range from a few years to more than a decade.

As changes occur in the technical environment, in user awareness, competitive offerings and market conditions, so do the requirements to develop additional product features and facilities. These development costs, together with maintenance, will continue well into the life of the product but will help extend its life. However there will come a stage when it is no longer economic to continue development and the product will stabilise, incurring little further expenditure and minimum maintenance. Eventually the market will become saturated, or the product obsolete or uncompetitive and revenues will decline. Two options are then open to the marketing manager, to:

- cut the price in order to tap the lower end of the market and prolong product life (common);

- raise the price to hasten the end of the product life and confine new customers to those with a higher need (rare).

Long before the final demise, the accumulated profit should be directed

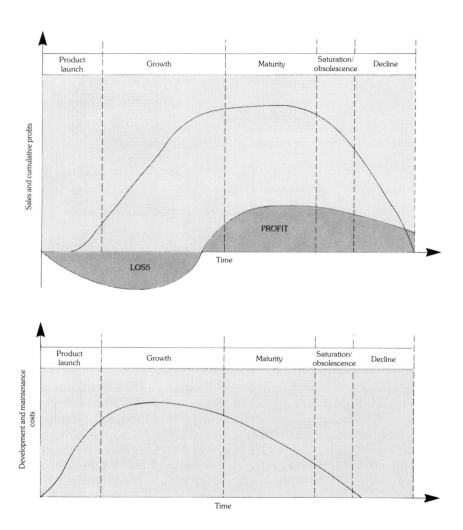

Figure 3.3   Software Product Life Cycle

towards the development of *replacement* products, which can be launched
on the established customer base and thus generate replacement revenues
(Figure 3.3).

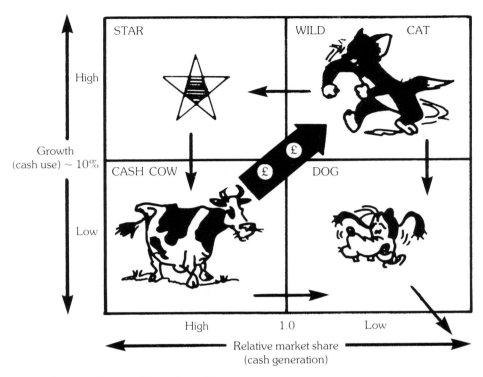

*Source: Boston Consulting Group.

Figure 3.4   BCG Growth/Share Matrix

The phases are very well expressed in the Boston Consulting Group (BCG) Growth/Share Matrix (Figure 3.4). In the BCG matrix, a new product *Wild Cat* can either fail and become a *Dog* or succeed and become a *Star*. Although still incurring high development costs the Star is also generating high revenues which stabilise as the product becomes a *Cash Cow* with lower costs. The steady profit generated by the Cash Cow helps finance the next Wild Cat venture until saturation is reached, when the product becomes a Dog and is withdrawn from the portfolio.

3.8.2 New Product Considerations

Before considerable development funds are allocated to a new product,

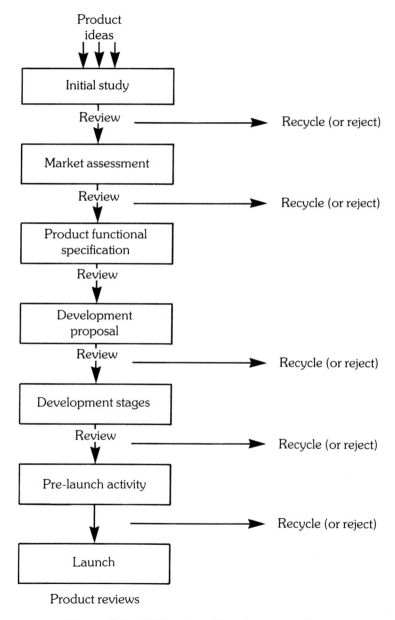

Figure 3.5   IT Product Development Cycle

marketing management must participate in a formal approach to determine by evaluation the potential profitability of that product. Experience of other industries shows that for every successful product reaching the market many do not and a high proportion incur losses. A formal approach will help avoid such situations by ensuring that the risks inherent in any new venture are monitored during the development stages.

Development Stages

The stages in a typical IT product's development cycle (Figure 3.5) are:

Initial Study

New product ideas or suggested product enhancements can derive from the company's own R&D, marketing or salespeople, technical support or development staff, or from the customers themselves.

It is normal for marketing departments to review the product line regularly in the search for new ideas. Marketing will gather sufficient data to undertake an initial study, covering:

— market potential;

— compatibility with company objectives;

— compatibility with product line;

— revenue and profit potential.

Many ideas flounder at this stage!

Market Assessment

The purpose of this stage is to confirm that the market opportunity is both real and quantifiable and to outline the main requirements of a product which will meet this opportunity.

The stage will conclude with a *market assessment report* (Table 3.5) which is circulated to all interested parties in the company. In particular the *outline product specification* may be used by the development group to provide an estimate of the likely development costs for inclusion in the business plan.

CONTENTS

1 MANAGEMENT SUMMARY

2 MARKET OPPORTUNITY

Market background

Market potential

Market demand

Competition

Marketing strategies

3 OUTLINE PRODUCT SPECIFICATION

Descriptive overview

Principal facilities and features

Operating environments and performance

Constraints and support environments

Enhancement potential

4 FINANCIAL JUSTIFICATION

Outline development costs

Pricing strategies and sales targets

Financial analysis

5 ACTION PLAN

Overview of project plan

Detailed plan for next stage

Resources and budget for next stage

APPENDICES

Table 3.5   Market Assessment Report

CONTENTS

1 GENERAL DESCRIPTION

   Introduction

   Outline specification

   Outline operating environment

   Terms and abbreviations

2 STANDARD FEATURES AND FACILITIES

   Features, described in detail, together with any interfaces
   (man—machine, hardware—software, software—operating system, etc)

3 OPTIONAL FEATURES AND FACILITIES

   As 2 for those features to be present or planned future options

4 DEVELOPMENT CONSIDERATIONS

   User and operating environment(s)

   Performance requirements

   Priorities of features and facilities

   User interface requirements

   Reliability and maintenance considerations

5 OTHER CONSIDERATIONS

   Timescale constraints

   Documentation considerations

   Further enhancement potential

Table 3.6   Product Functional Specification

This broad picture of the scale of investment required will allow management to decide whether or not to proceed further. It is quite possible for 25%–50% of such assessments to be rejected (or recycled for further study) at this stage.

Product Functional Specification

The output from this stage is a product specification (Table 3.6) written in terms of what features and facilities are required by the market in some order of priority. Some market research will have been undertaken to justify both requirements and priorities.

As in previous stages, although other parts of the organisation will be consulted for input, the task of preparing the specification is essentially a marketing responsibility.

Development Proposal

The development group can now study the product functional specification, decide its approach and estimate costs and timescales. From such estimates, the marketing group can complete the *business plan* (Table 3.7). Negotiation between the marketing and the development group will take place and some 'fine tuning' undertaken possibly to improve the specification or reduce development costs.

The risks having now been evaluated, the marketing group can submit the business plan to top management for approval. At this point comparatively little expenditure has been incurred. Once approval is given the real costs start in earnest.

Development Stages

The product is then developed against a plan and agreed timescales. In some cases, notably software products, a *prototype* is developed first. This can be used to confirm the specification at selected customer sites, invite comments and as a result iron out shortcomings in the product.

At the conclusion of the development stage an in-house version of the product should be tested against the product functional specification to check compliance.

Pre-launch Activity

In the meantime, the marketing group will be preparing for the product launch. In the software product arena, the pre-launch process will include the selection of 'beta test' sites, where the product can be fully evaluated in a user environment. The pre-release version of the product would thus be used to iron out bugs.

CONTENTS

1 MANAGEMENT SUMMARY

2 MARKET OPPORTUNITY
Market background
Market segments
Market potential
Market demand
Competition
Other market factors

3 PRODUCT REQUIREMENTS

Background/descriptive overview
Principal facilities, features, variations
User operating environments
Technical requirements
Enhancement potential
Competitive product evaluation

4 MARKETING STRATEGIES

Target market segments
Sales strategies
Product packaging
Advertising and promotion
Installation, support and maintenance
Product launch

5 FINANCIAL JUSTIFICATION

(Outline) development costs
Pricing considerations
Sales targets
Cost elements
Financial plan, payback, ROI

6 RISKS, EXPOSURES, DEPENDENCIES, ALTERNATIVES

7 ACTION PLAN

Planning phase
Development phase
Product introduction

APPENDICES

Table 3.7   Business Plan Proforma

	Action	Completion by	
		Target	**Actual**
In-house pre-release product accepted	Marketing/Development		
Beta test sites chosen	Marketing/Sales		
Draft product documentation available	Marketing		
Field support person trained	Marketing/Sales		
Beta test sites installed	Development/Sales		
Selling strategies agreed	Sales/Marketing		
Support philosophy agreed	Sales/Marketing		
Maintenance philosophy agreed	Sales/Technical support		
Data sheets prepared for printing	Marketing		
Brochures prepared for printing	Marketing		
Advertising space booked	Marketing		
Advertising copy prepared	Marketing		
Product licence documentation prepared	Marketing		
Beta test sites evaluated	Marketing/Development		
Business plan updated	Marketing		
PRE-LAUNCH REVIEW	All		
Arrange press conference, press release	Marketing		
Prepare sales presentations	Marketing/Sales		
Prepare sales demonstrations	Marketing/Technical support		
Print brochures, data sheets, manuals, etc	Marketing		
Confirm adverts and copy	Marketing		
Pre-launch sales training	Marketing/Sales		
Pre-launch support training	Technical support/ Development		
Set post-launch review criteria	Marketing/Sales		
PRODUCT LAUNCH	All		
POST-LAUNCH REVIEW		(6-12 months from launch)	

Table 3.8   Product Launch Checklist

For other products a period of *test marketing* – possibly within a single sales territory – may be undertaken to validate the marketing programme and product acceptability.

Product Launch

Finally the product is released with as much publicity as can be generated through press conferences, local exhibitions and advertising (Table 3.8). The product is now in the hands of the salesman!

Product Review

It is essential that the marketing group should monitor the progress of a new product in the first six months. Action may be required to keep the product on course or to respond to new market conditions. It is quite likely that two or more years may have passed since the product was first put forward as a development project. During this time many changes will have occurred in the market and in user awareness. Although such changes should have been monitored it is necessary to evaluate fully the enhancement progress to confirm the product's relevance to today's market.

3.9 BUYING BEHAVIOUR

3.9.1 Understanding the Buying Process

The final but nonetheless essential aspect of marketing management is a full understanding of the factors which influence the buyer. In Section 7.7.8 it will be seen that throughout the dialogue with a prospective customer, the professional salesman will react to *buying signals,* which reflect the six stages the buyer will go through.

In summary these are:

— *awareness* of need;

— gathering *knowledge* of products that could help;

— *liking* for particular features;

— *preference* for a supplier or product;

— *conviction* to proceed;

— *purchase* with formal documentation.

The salesman will seek out information during client meetings which will help him/her to understand buyer behaviour, such as:

— the prospect's buying procedure;

Buy phases	Buy classes		
	New task	Modified re-buy	Straight re-buy
1 Anticipation or recognition of a problem (need) and a general solution			
2 Determination of characteristics and quantity of needed item			
3 Description of characteristics and quantity of needed item			
4 Search for and qualification of potential sources			
5 Acquisition and analysis of proposals			
6 Evaluation of proposals and selection of supplier(s)			
7 Selection of an order routine			
8 Performance feedback and evaluation			

Table 3.9   The Manchester Polytechnic Buy Grid Analytical Framework for Industrial Buying Situations

- the personalities involved in the buying process;
- the stages at which they are involved;
- the influences they have on the decision;
- the rational and emotional factors which motivate them.

The marketing group will also recognise that if it is to *support* the salesman, it too will need to recognise the buying behaviour of the market. Thus all its efforts involved in the development of products, preparation and publicity will meet its customer's specifications at the earliest time in the buying process.

Some industrial marketing managers use *tools* such as the *Buy Grid Framework** to analyse each of the major customers and assess where marketing emphasis should be placed within the buying process (Table 3.9). This technique requires marketing to segregate its customers into three classes:

— *new task purchasers,* where the customer is buying a new product for the first time to meet a need;

— *re-buy purchasers,* where the customer is buying on a repeat order basis;

— *modified re-buy purchasers,* where the customer is now looking for enhancements, earlier delivery, better service or a lower price.

Such analysis of the target market helps marketing management meet users' specifications, avoid complacency and retain a satisfied customer base.

3.9.2 Buying Roles

The final aspect of buying behaviour is that of the roles played by different people, collectively termed the *buying centre.* Just as the salesmen must be aware of the part they each play in the buying equation, so also must their needs be reflected by marketing in all its activities. For example, the message in a sales brochure must address not only the person likely to make the buying decision but also the persons likely to *influence* that decision, notably, in IT circles, the *end-user.* The parties so identified comprise:

Gatekeepers

The gatekeeper is the person responsible for collecting data on IT equipment and services and for sending routine enquiries to potential suppliers. Although not necessarily a senior person, nor decision maker,

* Courtesy of Manchester Polytechnic, Faculty of Management and Business.

the extent of the gatekeeper's influence on purchasing should be sought.

Users

In IT such persons are deemed *end-users,* and as such employ the services of the IT department. Thus they are major *influencers,* whose needs can easily override other commercial considerations such as price.

Influencers

People who stimulate, inform, persuade or dissuade the decision makers at any stage in the buying process are deemed *influencers.* They are not readily identified since communications within an organisation are informal as well as formal. Sometimes they are *outside* the organisation. Key influencers in IT buying are:

- technical IT staff;

- senior management;

- end-users;

- some buyers;

- industry 'gurus'.

Buyers

The person placing the order may not necessarily be the decision maker nor the recommender. However the buyer is an *influencer* if only because he/she is the organisation's *purchasing professional.* The buyer might also be the individual who can *refer* the salesman to the decision maker.

Deciders

Clearly the key person in the buying process but not always easily found. Many sales have floundered through focusing attention on non-decision makers.

When the decision to buy is made by the consensus of a board or steering committee, the vital link in the buying chain is the *recommender.* The astute salesman will ascertain the success or otherwise of this person in gaining board approval of his or her previous recommendations. If the track record is poor then the other *key influencers* must be located and convinced.

Part 2
The Job

My business is to create

– William Blake

4 Selling Overview

4.1 ROLE OF THE IT SALESMAN

4.1.1 The Salesman

In his book *Selling Professional Services* Tony Davis makes the following points:

> "Freedom of choice, when selecting goods and services, is the basic driving force of the entire economy. Indirectly it has produced inventions, encouraged technical awareness and stimulated capital investment.
>
> From the very beginning of business these individual choices or buying decisions have been influenced materially by the personal sales and educational efforts of salesmen. Selling has been a dominant force in overcoming the natural resistance to change and will play an equally important role in the continuing growth and awareness of the future. It is not enough, when the customer desire is already there, for the salesman merely to supply a product or service. They must go beyond this to *create* additional wants and desires for our products and for the replacement of old products.
>
> The need for *creative* selling today is as great as it was over 100 years ago. If the world is to continue to progress towards a higher standard of living, products must be sold through the creative efforts of the salesman. Thus the whole concept of successful selling is centred around creativity. Creativity can be found in several areas, such as creating new uses for a product; and using different methods of developing customers."

In summary, Davis concludes that opportunities always exist for a salesman (through creativity) to prepare that which has not been done before, designing new networks, developing new sales strategies, each contributing to the collective knowledge in sales successes for future salesmen and establishing standards for what the company's product can do.

4.1.2 Selling Solutions

Broadly there are two groups of salespeople in the IT industry: those who sell solutions and those who sell consumable products and services. The job of the latter is usually highly structured in terms of who to see, what to do, how to do it and how to process the paperwork. Solution selling, often to groups, is more difficult and is probably one of the most skilled jobs in the profession of selling. Being far less structured it requires the salesman to compensate for a higher *refusal* rate and still achieve the overall sales objectives within a timescale. Solution selling is highly creative and offers the greater scope for self-expression and reward. In this book we are concerned with IT salespeople who sell *solutions*.

4.1.3 Responsibilities

The prime role of the IT salesman is to protect and increase the company's revenues in a profitable manner. Therefore within a defined territory – which could be based on geographical boundaries, industry type or product specialisation – the IT salesman will be responsible for:

- achieving the required sales target within an agreed timescale (normally one year), the spirit of the corporate objective and an acceptable level of expenditure (budget);

- providing feedback information to the company on all relevant matters;

- reporting accurately on the progress of all such activities;

- reflecting the company's image in all communications;

- conserving company resources;

- displaying company loyalty and knowledge;

- being perceived as well informed and reliable.

4.1.4 Tasks

The tasks necessary to discharge these responsibilities are covered fully in Chapters 7 and 8 but will include the following:

- acquaintance with corporate plan;
- preparation of an operational plan (strategic) to guarantee sufficient activity to generate the required level of sales in the year;
- provision of sufficient flexibility (tactical) to respond to sales opportunities;
- periodical reporting of progress: target and accurate forecasting by quarter/year;
- maintenance of territory records and promulgation of intelligence, especially market data and competitive activity;
- close attention to professional sales methods in all client dealings, with particular relevance to qualification criteria and sales presentation;
- attendance and contribution to training courses, conferences and progress meetings, such events providing timely updates on products, technology and sales methods;
- regular dialogue with support personnel;
- maintenance of all product and sales aids.

4.2 REWARDS

Generally the financial reward for selling information technology is high, as is the job's potential for satisfying the higher level needs of individuals.

4.2.1 Salary Levels

The comparison of salary levels in Table 4.1 was compiled from data contained in two pay/salary surveys conducted in 1987*. Since salaries are soon outdated, the actual amounts taken from the original surveys have been converted to points on a scale proportionate to the value of 100, the national average income for male employees. Exclusive of all perquisites, it shows that the income levels of IT salespeople compare favourably with those of the higher paid professions. As in other sectors, star performers will earn well in excess of the highest point on the scale. However the object of this exercise is to present a realistic comparison which is relevant to the majority of the IT sales population.

*The Times 80 Earnings Table; NCC, Salaries and Staff Issues in Computing.

Job	Related profession	Points value	Position
Senior airline captain	Airline pilot	406	1
Management consultant	Various	394	2
Taxation consultant	Accountancy	301	3
Surgeon	Medicine	285	4
IT salesman (distributed systems)	Selling	259	5
Branch manager	Banking	238	6
IT salesman (mainframe systems)	Selling	236	7
University professor	Academic	236	7
Reporter (national daily)	Journalism	220	9
Accountant (transport group)	Accountancy	217	10
Sales manager (transport group)	Selling	217	10
Engineering manager (chemicals)	Chemical engineering	212	12
Head of management services	Computing/various	208	13
IT salesman (software)	Selling	198	14
Plant manager	Engineering	189	15
IT salesman (microcomputers)	Selling	179	16
Systems analyst	Computing	171	17
Sales manager	Consumer products	170	18
Dispensing chemist	Pharmacy	167	19
Data processing manager	Computing	166	20
Sales manager (FMCG)	Selling	160	21
Solicitor (police authority)	Law	154	22
Senior teacher (mathematics)	Teaching	144	23
Sales engineer (electronics products)	Selling	142	24
Salesman (technical)	Selling	127	25
Salesman (consumer products)	Selling	118	26
Computer programmer	Computing	117	27
(national average for males)		(100)	
Social worker	Social services	90	28
Draughtsman	Engineering	87	29
Mechanic	Automotive	77	30
Zookeeper	Animal husbandry	70	31
Computer operator	Computing	69	32
(national average for females)		(66)	

*Source: *The Times* 80 Earnings Table, 1987; and NCC *Salaries and Staff Issues in Computing.*

Table 4.1   Comparison of Salary Levels in 1987*

4.2.2 Payment by Results

Although the remuneration schemes offered by IT suppliers are many and varied, most plans for sales personnel relate to payment by results. Thus earnings are usually a function of basic salary and incentive payment. Incentive payment is either a *commission* calculated as a percentage of the value of sales achieved, or *bonus* based on sales performance:target, or a combination of both commission and bonus.

The 'breaks' between basic salary and incentive payment can vary between companies and between different sales jobs. A remuneration scheme might operate as follows:

- the job evaluation process determines salary grades after appropriate consultation;

- the grade is subject to cost of living adjustment;

- the grade provides minimum and maximum levels, allowing scope for increases reflecting overall performance;

- a 'break' between basic salary and incentive bonus is set according to the nature of the job. For example:

Job	*Emphasis*	*Break*	
		Salary	*Bonus*
1 Territory sales	Secure new business	60	40
2 Major account sales	Develop accounts	80	20
3 Special task sales	Penetrate competitors' accounts	95	5

- in each case the scope for *attaining* or *exceeding* the salary level (100) will depend on sales performance:target.

4.2.3 On Target Earnings (OTE)

Many job advertisements quote 'OTE potential earnings *c* £*x*'. OTE is an acceptable principle of payment for salespeople provided that the sales target is realistic. If, for reasons of product quality, competitiveness, or availability or market saturation/territory size the target is unachievable then the OTE will not be realised.

4.2.4 Remuneration Packages

Recently there has been a trend towards the introduction of remuneration packages.

Such packages include perks such as company car, free private petrol, private health schemes, holidays abroad, and non-contributory pension plans. It is difficult to measure the real benefit of such perks, since they will vary in value between individuals. For example, if an employee attaches great importance to private health screening and would subscribe to it anyway then it is very valuable.

Another factor is that of tax levels. * Denis Crowe, *Income Data Services* (1987) suggests that:

> "By making certain presumptions (such as one's annual mileage being around 12,000) the value of a company car to its recipient can be categorised. For example, in 1987 an Austin Montego 1.6 l to someone paying income tax at 27% was worth an additional £3600 to his/her salary. To someone paying 40%, the same car was worth an additional £4200. At 50% a Rover Sterling 2.5 l would work out at £12,800."

Job applicants should understand fully the range and value of remuneration packages as well as the terms of salary and incentive bonus on offer.

4.3 TEAM SPIRIT

The IT salesman can be likened to a professional striker in football who plays *in* a team, but *for* a club. All involved in the club – directors, administrators, ground staff, supporters' club, doctor, physiotherapist, manager and coach – will be contributing to the success of the club by supporting the team in their various ways.

The player contributes to the success of the team and will be instrumental in scoring goals. He will be reliant upon the performance of his team mates and they with him in his endeavour to score more goals than the team's opponents in every match. Irrespective of his individual

*Source: Your just desserts: assessing them and getting them, the *Times* – 25 August 1987. ©Times Newspapers Ltd, 1987.

skill, the performance of the player on the field will depend *inter alia* on the indirect support provided by the club and the direct support of the other players.

In the case of the IT salesman, the club is the *company* and the team his *colleagues* in marketing and sales who provide sales support, technical support, guidance and coaching. The salesman should maintain excellent relationships with such colleagues at all levels and make his/her contribution where it counts – achieving sales goals.

4.4 ACHIEVING PROFESSIONALISM

Sales professionalism is achieved by blending personal qualities with knowledge and applying to the mixture well-proven sales methods.

4.4.1 Personal Qualities

If I were asked to describe a top salesman, I would suggest that he/she had an abundance of:

- presence;
- charm;
- confidence;
- empathy;
- creativity;
- enthusiasm;
- energy;
- communication skills;
- ability to achieve.

Many of these qualities are inherent but they can be developed through behavioural training and the *acquisition of knowledge*. For example, *empathy* is defined as the power to project one's personality into – and thus fully comprehend – the object of contemplation. In a sales situation the object of contemplation is the customer's needs and *proving the need* is an important step in the sales cycle. It involves asking the right questions. Empathising with the client is made much simpler if the salesman has a sound knowledge of the characteristics and organisation of the client's business. Recognition of personal qualities is fundamental to IT sales staff selection and is discussed further in Section 5.2.4.

4.4.2 Knowledge

Knowledge is a rich storehouse for the glory of the Creator and the relief of man's estate.

– Francis Bacon

Knowledge in the IT business, like any other, is a function of two attributes – education and experience. Since IT is a highly dynamic subject, the practitioner must keep abreast of technology change. In IT selling this is achieved through continuous training. In Section 3.9.2 we considered the parts played by different people in the buying process, namely the gatekeeper, user, influencer, buyer and decider. Understanding buyer behaviour is an important requirement of any professional salesman but especially so in solution selling. Thus in approaching these different people, the IT salesman must understand their *role* and their *needs* before proposing solutions. This will require a sound knowledge of:

– types of organisation and the way they transact business;

– information technology and its capabilities in meeting their needs;

– the characteristics of mainstream computer environments;

– one's own products and services;

– the strengths and weaknesses of competitors;

– sales methods which have stood the test of time.

Consider an IT salesperson whose main product is a Fourth Generation Language (4GL). Let us suppose that the company's marketing support group has been running a mailing campaign targeted at engineering companies in the manufacturing sector and has received a response from an aircraft component manufacturer asking for further details. During the first meeting he has established a *need* by the DP manager to reduce the pressure on his or her (already overworked) department. The DP manager feels that this would be best achieved by providing end-users with the *means* to develop their own application programs. His knowledge will tell him that at present there are five distinct techniques for implementing the man–machine interface – the means by which the user accesses the software development power of the 4GL – namely, spreadsheet, database, form filling, menu selection and procedural language.

His product uses the form filling interface and he has ascertained that the competition is active, using the database interface technique. His knowledge of sales method and buyer behaviour will tell him that before he can close the sale, he must *prove the need* for his product and achieve company, product and personal *credibility* from the prospect. It will also tell him that (in this case) the decision maker is the DP manager but that the decision to buy will be influenced by the end-users. Further investigation – part of 'proving the need' – reveals that the real pressure on the DP manager has derived from the production director who requires a system that will enable him to respond quickly to sales enquiries. This involves the development of a program that will calculate the effect of accepting an order on the forward load of the assembly and machine shop departments under his control.

In a meeting with the production director his knowledge of production methods enables him to understand the latter's needs and he is able to show that the form filling interface is ideally suited to the situation. He reinforces his point by prototyping the system in a demonstration. The *influencer* has confidence in the salesman's clear understanding of the company's needs and becomes his ally. Convincing the decision maker is then relatively straightforward. Of course the next prospect might be an insurance company, where a broad understanding of policy file mainte-nance, renewals generation and investment valuation, together with relational database techniques would do much to help close the sale.

In conclusion, no single salesperson can expect to possess a detailed knowledge of all types of business, IT, or the environments of IBM, Unisys, ICL, DEC and other major computer manufacturers; but evidence of a good *all round* knowledge will do much to convince those involved in the buying process that solutions to their problems will be in good hands. The levels of knowledge required in the business, IT, and sales method areas are discussed further in Chapters 6 and 7.

5 Recruitment

5.1 SOURCES OF CANDIDATES

Applicants for IT sales positions derive normally from five sources and age groups:

Source	Broad age group
IT professionals employed in user installations	25–40
IT professionals employed by suppliers	25–40
Sales professionals in other disciplines	25–35
Business or technical professionals	25–40
Trainees	21–25

The skills acquired by such candidates through education, experience, training and professional qualification will vary considerably. Much of the knowledge assembled by most of the groups will be invaluable in the IT sales environment. The qualified accountant should have no problems with business practice, nor should the young business graduate from the polytechnic or university school of management. The systems analyst will understand both business needs and computer applications – an irresistible combination when selling IT solutions. The sales professional will understand sales techniques and territory management. The IT professional working in a supplier environment will doubtless know much about the application of IT solutions and the nature of computing. However, none of these groups will possess the *overall* knowledge preferred by IT suppliers in selling IT solutions to the business world.

The training required to bridge knowledge gaps is both costly and time consuming. In the larger companies, much of the training costs will be

Candidates	Organisations (business)	Business practice	Specialist business areas	Systems options	Systems analysis	Systems design	Data organisation	Database	Software tools	Languages	Operating systems	Utilities (software)	Assemblers	Application programs	Data communications	Mainframe environments	Distributed environments	Open systems	Office automation	Compatibility	Company products	Sales method	Report writing	Presentations
IT user environment																								
Systems analyst/designer	C	C	A	C	C	C	A	A	A	A	A	A	A	A	A	A	A	C	A				C	A
Analyst programmer	A	A	A	C	C	C	C	C	C	C	C	C	C	A	C	C	A	A	A				A	A
Business analyst	C	C	A	C	C	A	A	A					A	A									C	C
Programmer	A	A	A	A	A	A	C	A	A	C	C	C	C	C	A	C	A	C	A	A			A	A
Systems programmer	A	A		A	A	A	C	C	C	C	C	C	C	A	C	C	C	C	A	C			A	A
Software engineer	A	A		A	C	C	C	C	C	C	C	A	A	C	C	C	C	A	A				A	A
Network designer	A	A	A	C	A	A	A	C	A	A	C	A	A	C	C	C	C	C					A	A
Database designer	C	C	A	C	C	C	C	C	C	C	C	C	A	C	C	A	C	A					C	A
IT supplier environment																								
Salesperson	C	C	C	A	A	A	C	C	C	C	C	A	C	C	C	A	C	C			C		C	C
Pre-sales support consultants	A	A	A	C	A	A	C	C	C	C	C	A	A	C	C	C	C	C	C		A		A	A
Post-sales support consultants	A	A	A	A	C	A	A	C	C	C	C	C	A	C	C	C	C	C	C		A		A	A
Trainer	A	C	A	C	C	C	C	C	A	C	C	C	C	A	C	C	C	C	C				A	C
Systems programmer	A	A		A	A	A	C	C	C	C	C	C	C	A	C	C	C	C	A	C			A	A
Marketing support consultants	A	A	A	A	A	A	A	A	A	A	A	A		A	A	A	A	A	A		A		C	A
Other industries																								
Professional salesman		A	A																		C		C	C
Business/technical professions																								
Accountant	C	C	A	A	A	A	A						A	A				A					C	A
Engineer	A	A	C											A									C	A
Line manager	C	C	A	A	A	A	A							A				A					C	C
Trainees																								
Business graduate	C	C	A	A	A	A	A	A		A	A	A	A	A	A	A		A			A		C	A
Computer science graduate	A	A		A	A	A	C	C	C	C	C	C	C	A	C	C	C	A	A	C			A	A
Other graduates																							A	A
Young business trainee	A	A		A		A												A			A		A	A
'A' level school leaver																							A	A
Standard for job																								
Ideal	C	C	B	C	B	B	B	C	C	C	C	C	B	C	C	C	C	C	C	C	C	C	C	C
Minimum	B	B	A	B	B	B	B	B	B	B	B	B	B	B	B	B	B	B	B	B	C	C	C	C

Key: C = comprehensive knowledge
 B = basic knowledge
 A = appreciation

Table 5.1   Relevant Skills for IT Salespeople

borne by the new employer, since such IT suppliers recognise the potentially high returns from the investment. However candidates themselves should understand their knowledge weaknesses and make time to redress the balance by independent study.

5.1.1 Relevant Skills

Table 5.1 attempts to quantify the relevance of the various skills acquired by the candidate classes to the requirements of the IT selling job. Some candidates will have knowledge levels in some areas which are in excess of the standards required for the job. All will require *some* training.

Bearing in mind that without the relevant *personal qualities* none of the candidates would be likely to succeed in IT selling, the folllowing general comments are offered in respect of candidate classes.

5.1.2 IT Professionals

Those coming from IT user environments will be strong in IT methods and in understanding business needs. Systems analysts and designers are particularly powerful candidates and will already have experience of 'selling' their solutions in house. Support consultants already working for IT suppliers are also prime material for IT sales appointments and will have had the additional exposure to sales negotiation. Systems programmers will have a deep understanding of utilities and other systems software so essential in specialist software companies.

5.1.3 Business/Technical Professionals

These candidates will have acquired a high level of credibility in their various disciplines which is of paramount importance when *proving the need* to a prospective client.

5.1.4 Trainees

Although lacking in experience, young trainees have a high capacity to absorb knowledge fast and an abundance of energy in applying such skills. Furthermore they are unlikely to be inhibited by outdated methods or conventions.

5.2 SELECTION CRITERIA

The *final* decision maker in the appointment of IT salespeople is usually the sales manager. Before interviewing the shortlisted candidates the following steps will have been taken:

5.2.1 Job Specification

Responsibility: Sales manager

A specification will be necessary for every sales appointment from trainee salesman to national accounts management. It will include a summary of the tasks (outlined in Section 4.1.4) and particulars of territory/specialisation boundaries.

5.2.2 Job Advertisement

Responsibility: Personnel manager

In line with both the job specification and corporate conditions of employment, the personnel manager will draft an advertisement or alternatively arrange for a specialist recruitment agency to undertake the work. The advertisement will be placed in either the national dailies/Sunday supplements, IT trade press, or professional journals – possibly all four.

5.2.3 Response Filter

Responsibility: Personnel manager or recruitment agency

The personnel manager/agency will receive and acknowledge all applications/CVs. The applications will first be compared factually, in terms of the relevance of attributes claimed by candidates through education and experience, against the job specification. Unsuitable candidates will receive a prompt and courteous letter explaining that on this occasion they have been unsuccessful. Potential candidates will be invited to attend an interview.

5.2.4 First Interview

Responsibility: Personnel manager/recruitment agency

Generally this interview has a five-fold objective, to:

- obtain confirmation and expansion of education and experience;

- gain a broad measure of the candidate's interest;

- explain more fully the nature of the job;

			Low				STENS					High			
Scale	RS	SS	1	2	3	4	5	6	7	8	9	10	**RELATIONSHIPS WITH PEOPLE**	
R1			•	•	•	•	•	•	•	•	•	•	**Persuasive –** Enjoys selling, changes opinions of others, convincing with arguments, negotiates	Assertive
R2			•	•	•	•	•	•	•	•	•	•	**Controlling –** Takes charge, directs, manages, organises, supervises others	
R3			•	•	•	•	•	•	•	•	•	•	**Independent –** Has strong views on things, difficult to manage, speaks up, argues, dislikes ties	
R4			•	•	•	•	•	•	•	•	•	•	**Outgoing –** Fun loving, humorous, sociable, vibrant, talkative, jovial	Gregarious
R5			•	•	•	•	•	•	•	•	•	•	**Affiliative –** has many friends, enjoys being in groups, likes companionship, shares things with friends	
R6			•	•	•	•	•	•	•	•	•	•	**Socially confident –** Puts people at ease, knows what to say, good with words	
R7			•	•	•	•	•	•	•	•	•	•	**Modest –** Reserved about achievements, avoids talking about self, accepts others, avoids trappings of status	Empathy
R8			•	•	•	•	•	•	•	•	•	•	**Democratic –** Encourages others to contribute, consults, listens and refers to others	
R9			•	•	•	•	•	•	•	•	•	•	**Caring –** Considerate to others, helps those in need, sympathetic, tolerant	
			1	2	3	4	5	6	7	8	9	10	**THINKING STYLE**	
T1			•	•	•	•	•	•	•	•	•	•	**Practical –** Down-to-earth, likes repairing and mending things, better with the concrete	Fields of use
T2			•	•	•	•	•	•	•	•	•	•	**Data rational –** Good with data, operates on facts, enjoys assessing and measuring	
T3			•	•	•	•	•	•	•	•	•	•	**Artistic –** Appreciates culture, shows artistic flair, sensitive to visual arts and music	
T4			•	•	•	•	•	•	•	•	•	•	**Behavioural –** Analyses thoughts and behaviour, psychologically minded, likes to understand people	
T5			•	•	•	•	•	•	•	•	•	•	**Traditional –** Preserves well proven methods, prefers the orthodox, disciplined, conventional	Abstract
T6			•	•	•	•	•	•	•	•	•	•	**Change oriented –** Enjoys doing new things, seeks variety, prefers novelty to routine, accepts changes	
T7			•	•	•	•	•	•	•	•	•	•	**Conceptual –** Theoretical, intellectually curious, enjoys the complex and abstract	
T8			•	•	•	•	•	•	•	•	•	•	**Innovative –** Generates ideas, shows ingenuity, thinks up solutions	
T9			•	•	•	•	•	•	•	•	•	•	**Forward planning –** Prepares well in advance, enjoys target setting, forecasts trends, plans projects	Structure
T10			•	•	•	•	•	•	•	•	•	•	**Detail conscious –** Methodical, keeps things neat and tidy, precise, accurate	
T11			•	•	•	•	•	•	•	•	•	•	**Conscientious –** Sticks to deadlines, completes jobs, perseveres with routine, likes fixed schedules	
			1	2	3	4	5	6	7	8	9	10	**FEELINGS AND EMOTIONS**	
F1			•	•	•	•	•	•	•	•	•	•	**Relaxed –** Calm, relaxed, cool under pressure, free from anxiety, can switch off	Anxieties
F2			•	•	•	•	•	•	•	•	•	•	**Worrying –** Worry when things go wrong, keyed-up before important events, anxious to do well	
F3			•	•	•	•	•	•	•	•	•	•	**Tough minded –** Difficult to hurt or upset, can brush off insults, unaffected by unfair remarks	
F4			•	•	•	•	•	•	•	•	•	•	**Emotional control –** Restrained in showing emotions, keeps feelings back, avoids outbursts	Controls
F5			•	•	•	•	•	•	•	•	•	•	**Optimistic –** Cheerful, happy, keeps spirits up despite setbacks	
F6			•	•	•	•	•	•	•	•	•	•	**Critical –** Good at probing the facts, sees the disadvantages, challenges assumptions	
F7			•	•	•	•	•	•	•	•	•	•	**Active –** Has energy, moves quickly, enjoys physical exercise, doesn't sit still	
F8			•	•	•	•	•	•	•	•	•	•	**Competitive –** Plays to win, determined to beat others, poor loser	
F9			•	•	•	•	•	•	•	•	•	•	**Achieving –** Ambitious, sets sights high, career centred, results orientated	Energies
F10			•	•	•	•	•	•	•	•	•	•	**Decisive –** Quick at conclusions, weighs things up rapidly, may be hasty, takes risks	
D1			•	•	•	•	•	•	•	•	•	•	**Consistency**	

PERCENTILES	1	4	11	23	40	60	77	89	96	99	**Norms used:** Professional and Managerial Group

Table 5.2 Saville & Holdsworth Profile Chart

  — assess the candidate's general qualities;

  — select a shortlist.

The interview may be helped by the use of occupational testing, including:

  — *Tests of ability or aptitude for IT*

    These include numeric reasoning, verbal reasoning, spatial ability,
    speed and accuracy. Candidates can be measured against, say, the
    'graduate' population.

  — *Tests of personality*

    These allow for a measure of different character traits such as
    persuasiveness, control, decisiveness, change orientation and com-
    petitiveness.

The profile chart in Table 5.2 was developed by Saville and Holdsworth
and is designed to assess 30 different character traits. However the
assessment of personal qualities is the forte of the skilled personnel
manager or recruitment specialist, who is highly trained in interview
techniques.

5.2.5 Shortlist Interview

Responsibility: Sales manager

The final shortlist of candidates will be interviewed by the sales manager
who will be giving his personal assessment. Much of this will be concerned
with the candidate's track record, potential for 'fitting into the team' and
the *courage* to accept refusal but 'bounce back' for the next opportunity.
As Franz Klammer so aptly put it: "If you want to win an Olympic Gold you
have to take the line of a *tiger,* not a chicken".

6 The Sales Trainee

6.1 INDUCTION

In a sense *all* new IT sales appointees, irrespective of background and experience are *trainees*. All will require familiarisation with the company, its *modus operandi,* people and products. This should be covered by an induction programme.

6.1.1 Objective

The aim of the induction programme is to prepare the new appointee for productive work as early as possible without jeopardising the quality of representation. The period of induction is unlikely to be less than five weeks, being a mixture of lecture sessions, private reading and practical work usually at the branch office. For some highly experienced incumbents the induction programme will provide all the initial training needed before appointment to a territory. For many, however, further training will be necessary to fill the knowledge gaps referred to in Section 5.1.

Figure 6.1 illustrates the point that those with relevant skills can by-pass sections of the complete training schedule. The inexperienced trainee, possibly a recent graduate, will require a longer 'apprenticeship' and is unlikely to gain full territory sales status in less than two years. During this period such trainees are likely to develop their skills as either assistant salesmen, customer services officers or branch assistants. Some may be employed in a marketing or sales support role. Under the guidance of experienced personnel they will build knowledge and attend courses, accepting greater levels of responsibility over time.

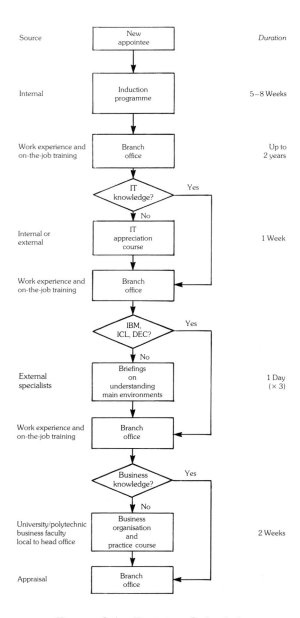

Figure 6.1   Training Schedule

It should be borne in mind that training is a *continuous* process and *all* sales staff, irrespective of seniority should be prepared to participate in regular programmes arranged by the training manager. The dynamic nature of IT demands frequent updating and all salespeople require regular reminders of the most effective sales methods.

6.1.2 Induction Programme

The induction programme should cover the major topics given in Table 6.1.

Week no	Duration (variable)	Topic	Location	Direction
1	2 Days	Local office familiarisation	Branch	Branch manager
	2 Days	Marketing group organisation	Head office	(Sales) training manager
	1 Day	Consolidation	Branch	Self
2	5 Days	Product training	Head office	(Sales) training manager
3	5 Days	On-the-job training	Branch	Branch manager, senior salesperson
4	5 Days	Company induction	Head office	(Sales) training manager, personnel manager
5	5 Days	On-the-job training	Branch	Branch manager, senior salesperson

Table 6.1   Induction Programme Topics

6.1.3 Key Topics

Emphasis should be given to the following:

Local Office Familiarisation

In the two days allocated, the branch manager should explain branch organistion and objectives, territorial divisions, personalities, local support services, and links to head office. The trainee will endeavour to meet all branch personnel.

Marketing Group Organisation

A balanced syllabus should comprise:

Perspective

How marketing and sales fit into the overall company structure.

Objectives

How marketing helps achieve the company's revenue targets, retain and develop customers, promote the company's image, and gather intelligence.

Functions

What marketing does:

- market research and access to information;
- market planning through information databases;
- marketing support via promotions and campaigns, publicity materials and brochures, public relations, product marketing executives, product trials and beta tests;
- sales support;
  - levels of technical pre/post-sales support, technical manuals, how to get help;
- sales administration:
  - procedures, disciplines, contracts,
  - order processing,

- options and prices,
- bonus scheme;

— sales organisation:

- main regions and franchises,
- national accounts,
- specialist areas/agencies,
- international operations/agencies,
- planning,
- reporting,
- conferences and progress meetings.

Product Training

For each major product or service, the induction programme should cover:

— Brief history:	Product overview
— Technical appreciation:	Features and benefits
— Successful sales:	Benefits quantified
— Practical usage:	Case studies
— Competition:	Features and shortcomings
— Standard presentation:	Demonstration sequence

Company Induction

Ideally this course should be attended on the earliest possible occasion, but since it is normally available to *all* new staff the training will depend on getting sufficient people together to mount the syllabus. Company induction should cover:

— company history, milestones and achievements;

— corporate identity;

— organisation;

- main activities:
  - research and development,
  - production,
  - operations,
  - marketing and sales;
- management services:
  - financial,
  - legal,
  - secretarial,
  - office services,
  - administration and personnel;
- staff facilities:
  - conditions of service,
  - health and safety,
  - union membership,
  - sports and social,
  - restaurant.

On-the-job Training

The prime responsibility of a sales manager and especially the field sales manager covering a region or branch is to *achieve sales objectives through* rather than *for* his or her salespeople. In order to build and maintain a salesteam which is stable, productive and satisfied, the branch manager will need to carry out four specific functions:

- train and develop *new* salespeople;
- continue to develop *experienced* salespeople;
- appraise and evaluate their performance;
- motivate them to achieve sales targets.

Thus the two ingredients for success are leadership and training – especially in the field. If a manager cannot *train* (and so develop skills), he cannot *manage*.

On-the-job training involves joint visits to customers and prospective customers with the trainee taking an increasingly active role in the negotiations over a period of time, and immediate discussion with the sales manager after each visit. Such sessions are dubbed *kerbside counselling* but are a well-proven means of becoming a sales professional.

6.2 TRAINING

Once established in the region or branch the trainee salesman will require further training during the first year and this will be mixed with practical experience and continuous on-the-job training with either the branch manager or senior salesperson. The courses to be attended will vary according to his/her knowledge gaps but the following should be considered.

6.2.1 Formal Sales Training

The best environment is a sales training workshop, intensive and highly interactive and located well away from office distractions. It should be limited to 12 participants from the sales staff. Topics should include:

- components of the sales cycle;
- prospect qualification;
- recognising business opportunities;
- account management;
- territory operation;
- presenting benefits;
- presenting proposals for change;
- handling objections;
- level selling;
- understanding the needs of industry sectors.

The use of interactive case studies involving the company's products and the presentation of proposals through syndicates will test technical, business knowledge and behavioural skills.

6.2.2 Advanced Presentation Skills

The aims of this type of workshop, limited to eight delegates, are to provide salespeople with professional presentation and teaching skills which enable them to pass on their technical knowledge and experience. Again the workshop will be highly participative, involving at least two presentations per delegate, one of which should be prepared prior to the event. Essential subjects comprise:

- course objectives;

- subject analysis;

- session structuring and design;

- presentation planning;

- selection, design and use of visual aids;

- presentation of documentation;

- effective speaking techniques;

- dealing with questions;

- audience involvement and control;

- the 'professional' approach.

Such topics would be covered in three days.

6.2.3 Information Technology

Any self-respecting IT salesperson will make time to learn more about the technology, via evening classes, correspondence courses or private reading. Indeed many excellent text books are available in paperback form.

The salesman should not rely entirely on his/her own employer to be the sole provider of IT knowledge. However many suppliers do include IT in the training programme. Subsequent success in the sales arena will depend heavily on one's understanding of the subject and thus, through a combination of company training and private study the IT sales trainee should aim to be fluent in the following:

- Input-process-output

- History of computing

- Hardware, software

and the central processor
- Database
- Processing methods
- Real-time processing
- Data capture
- Data input
- Methods of output
- Backing storage
- Direct Access
- File structure
- File organisation
- People in computing
- Documentation standards
- How programs work
- Programming languages
- Programming applications
- Future trends

This syllabus will provide the inexperienced trainee with an appreciation of the *nature* of IT. It should be augmented by a series of training modules covering the principles in more depth, including:

- Office automation:

  Components

  Communications options

  Justification

  Planning and implementation

- Using computers
  (user viewpoint):

  Effective uses of IT

  Information storage
  and retrieval

	Programs (software)
	IT developments
	Project management
— System selection (user viewpoint):	Introduction to systems analysis
	Hardware application
	Specification of requirements
	Selection criteria
	Evaluation of proposals
— Data transmission:	Elements of data transmission
	Communications principles and modulation techniques
	Communications hardware
	Line control and interfaces
	UK exchange lines and private circuits
	UK data transmission facilities
	Errors, failures and reliability
	Public data networks
— Local area networks:	Overview
	LAN applications
	LAN implementation
	Networking
	The PABX alternative
	Choosing a LAN
	LAN standards

	LAN gateways
	LAN products
— Packet switching (extension of data transmission):	Current methods, including public switched network, private circuit operation, line control, interfacing, error control, multiplexers and concentrators in the packet switched environment
	Meeting users' requirements
— Database:	Concepts
	Design
	Administration
	Software and languages

Depending upon the company, its products and particular market niche, some salespeople will require far more IT training in subjects such as software engineering, real-time systems design, and expert systems.

6.2.4 Business Organisation and Practice

Many excellent courses are offered by the universities, polytechnics and business schools, leading to degrees in management, business and the 'ultimate' MBA. Graduates from such faculties make excellent candidates for responsible positions in the IT industry, including sales and marketing jobs. Candidates with business experience as accountants, systems designers and other professions will also have a sound knowledge of business practice. For those without such knowledge it is imperative that they become acquainted with the following *minimum* understanding of business if they are to empathise with IT decision makers:

— Business organisations:	Manufacturing industry
	Distribution industry
	Services industry

— Public organisations: Central government

                                              Local government

                                              Utilities

— Business functions: Research and development

                                                Production

                                              Marketing and sales

                                              Finance

                                              Management services

— Marketing concepts: Environment

                                                Market planning

                                              Market research

                                              Product life cycle

— Marketing mix: Product pricing

                                              Advertising and promotion

                                              Distribution

                                              Direct selling

— Background to finance: Budgeting

                                              Cash behaviour

                                              Pricing

                                              Cash flow analysis

                                              Working capital management

                                              Financial statements

— Organisational behaviour: Components of individual
                                                  behaviour

                                              Motivation process

                                              Individual behaviour in
                                              organisations

6.2.5 Mainstream Systems Environments

Many of today's IT installations include, or are likely to include hardware and software products from more than one supplier. Therefore IT decision makers will raise questions with IT suppliers on issues of compatibility and how such suppliers can integrate their products with the environments of the major computer manufacturers, such as IBM, DEC and ICL.

In order to market successfully in these situations the IT salesman requires an understanding of the products, standards, protocols, and terminology of such environments. Of particular relevance is a broad appreciation of the major mainframe and distributed systems, operating systems, transaction processing software, database management systems, open systems interconnection, and the various levels of plug compatibility.

6.3 APPRAISAL

6.3.1 Annual Appraisal

The well-organised IT supplier company will doubtless operate an annual appraisal scheme for *all* staff. The objective and purpose of the corporate appraisal scheme will comprise:

Assessment of performance in terms of:

- work knowledge;

- quality and quantity;

- personality, relationships, involvement and motivation;

- ability to communicate;

- capacity for constructive thought;

- managerial ability;

- direction of others.

Recommendations such as:

- special training;

- change in work utilisation;

- promotion.

6.3.2 On-the-job Appraisal

In addition to the annual appraisal, regional or branch sales managers will wish to assess the performance of their staff in real situations with customers. This is particularly important for sales trainees as part of the on-the-job training discussed in Section 6.1.3.

Following each customer/potential customer visit the regional manager should assess his sales trainee on the following lines:

— *Visit to potential customer* where the prospects for business are *unknown*. In this situation the manager will consider:

Did the trainee:

- Understand and define the objective of the meeting?

- Make an impression in the first 30 seconds?

- Show personal and corporate credibility?

- Qualify the prospects for business?

- Achieve the objective of the visit?

— *Visit to potential customer* where the prospects for business have been *identified* and *qualified*. In this scenario, involving the *presentation* of a proposal, the manager will be asking:

Did the trainee:

- Make an impact in his/her opening statement?

- Summarise his/her objective, background to the case, solution?

- Show a full understanding of the client's needs/and 'own' strengths?

- Describe clearly 'our' solution without recourse to jargon?

- Present costs and *savings*?

- Explain and *relate* the benefits of 'our' solution?

- Describe comprehensively and reassuringly the proposed implementation plan?

- Summarise the proposal again?

- Seek a decision?

Only if he or she is satisfied on all counts will the manager pronounce the trainee as 'fit to fly'.

Clearly without the mix of knowledge, experience and personal qualities the new trainee is unlikely to be ready to accept responsibility for a territory. However he/she may well have demonstrated an ability to work in a sales environment under supervision and a potential to accept promotion within, say, one year.

7 The Territory Salesman

7.1 TERRITORY MANAGEMENT

7.1.1 The Nature of a Territory

In Chapter 5 we discussed the role, responsibilities and key tasks of the IT salesman within a clearly defined territory. It is important to appreciate the nature of a sales territory and the salesman's commitment to its *management*. The true professional will liken the territory to that of owning one's business, but without the problem of raising capital. After all in most companies, territories so defined become the *exclusive* domain of the salesperson. Familiarisation with a territory may take up to two years to develop, during which time he/she will get to know the organisations which comprise the market, personalities, growth patterns, regional development strategies and so forth. The greater the familiarity, the higher the potential for sound planning of territory operations and for higher sales levels.

7.1.2 Types of Territory

Generally territories divide into three classes:

— geographical;
— specialist;
— vertical.

Geographically bounded territories can be defined accurately through the national postcodes (Table 7.1).

Specialist territories comprise certain *types* of organisation, usually major establishments, irrespective of geographical location. Examples include:

— government: Ministry of Defence;

Judith Brown Territory Code: AB	
Postcode	**Areas covered**
WC2	London
SW	London
KT	Kingston-upon-Thames, including towns below:
	Ashtead, Byfleet, Chertsey, Chessington, Cobham, East Molesey, Effingham, Epsom, Kingston, Leatherhead, New Maldon, Surbiton, Tadworth, Thames Ditton, Walton-on-Thames, West Byfleet, West Molesey, Weybridge, Worcester Park
SM	Sutton, including towns below:
	Banstead, Carshalton, Morden, Sutton, Wallington
RH	Redhill, including towns below:
	Billinghurst, Burgess Hill, Crawley, Dorking, East Grinstead, Gatwick, Godstone, Haywards Heath, Horley, Horsham, Oxtead, Pulborough, Redhill, Reigate
BN	Brighton, including towns below:
	Arundel, Brighton, Eastbourne, Hailsham, Hassocks, Hove, Lancing, Lewes, Littlehampton, Newhaven, Polegate, Seaford, Shoreham, Worthing
	Exclusions All government (inc MoD) establishments All public utilities All national accounts as scheduled

Table 7.1   Example Territory Definition

- government: all other ministries;

- public utilities: all gas, electricity, water boards, regional health authorities, hospitals;

- major industrials: British Telecom, ICI, Shell, British Petroleum, British Aerospace, Rolls Royce, etc.

Vertical territories can relate to specific classes of industry, irrespective of geographical location such as:

- all local authorities;

- all joint stock banks;

- all building societies;

- all stockbrokers.

Vertical territories can also relate to specific types of systems, for example:

- all ICL VME (operating system) users;

- all IBM CICS (transaction processing system) users.

7.1.3 Company Communications

It is essential that *all* communications between different parts of the company and organisations within a territory be copied to the territory salesman. All staff should understand that the salesman is the *prime* representative of the company in a territory and in this capacity needs to know everything that is going on. Failure to give information will undermine his/her authority in the eyes of customers.

7.1.4 Managing the Territory

Although the territory salesperson may not have the responsibility for managing other staff, he/she is nonetheless involved in work scheduling and the use of resources. The most important resource is *time,* one's own time generally, but also including the time spent by support staff in pre- and post-sales activities. Other managerial skills applied by the territory salesman include planning, forecasting and reporting – all contributing to the basic objective of achieving sales targets.

7.2 TERRITORY PLANNING

One very effective way to plan a territory operation for the year ahead is for the salesman to produce an *operational plan* in accordance with a set of *planning guidelines* set by the branch/regional manager.

7.2.1 Operational Plan Guidelines

The guidelines should include:

Planning Scenario

This will be an overview of the year ahead in terms of the likely economic climate, company growth plans, key development areas, planned marketing promotions, new product releases and opportunities for *value added* activities.

Responsibilities List

The main responsibilities assigned to the salesman comprise:

— achievement of a sales target by products and in total;

— customer servicing and account development;

— effective response to all sales enquiries;

— regular period reports on activity, secured business and prospects;

— reasonable adherence to the operational plan.

Proposed Format

The guidelines should ask the salesman to submit his/her plans for the year ahead in the following format:

— list of geographic sectors into which he/she has decided to divide the territory with economy of travelling time in mind;

— list of all customers within each sector, suitably annotated to indicate size, business potential and, where leased products are concerned, the licence renewal dates;

— list of other organisations within each sector which have the *potential* to become customers.

Schedule of Planned Sales Visits

This is the most important part of the operational plan, requiring the salesman to *analyse* the territory; to identify product sales potential; and to produce a *planned schedule* of visits. The required level of activity (sales visits) will take account of:

— the number of unit sales required for each product;

— conversion ratios from:

  • cold visit to qualified prospect,

  • qualified prospect to product trial/sales proposal,

  • proposal to firm order.

In preparing the schedule of planned sales visits, the salesman will assume the following cycle:

Event	Assessed by
List of territory potential	Salesman
Qualified prospects	Salesman/support staff
Trials/proposals	Salesman/support staff
Commitment	Salesman

Conversion rates *might* be assessed as:

Qualified prospect to trial/proposal	40%
Trial/proposal to order	70%

The schedule will be divided into (13) accounting periods, each of four weeks, the object being to produce as even a spread of visits as possible in proportion to the distribution of customers/prospects with due regard to travelling time. The schedule should ensure that no part of the territory remains unvisited for long periods and that time is available to follow up sales leads as they occur (ie *unplanned visits*). During the ensuing year the planned visit schedule could be overridden by unplanned but *higher priority* visits in response to serious sales enquiries. In this event the unplanned visit would also be recorded in the period visit report (Figure 7.1) and those planned calls which had not taken place would be rescheduled for later in the year.

Salesman_____ Territory code_____ Period_____

PLANNED VISITS Company name	Visit type by product	M/C used	Sector	Comments
1				
2				
3				
4				
5				
6				
7				
8				
9				
10				
11				
12				
13				
14				
15				
UNPLANNED VISITS				
1				
2				
3				
4				
5				
6				
7				
8				
9				
10				

Actual visits completed: Planned   =
                         Unplanned =
                         _____
                         Total
                         _____

Figure 7.1   Period Visit Report

Strategic Sales Training Ltd (SST) in its sales training workshops warns of the 'halo effect' caused through a salesman's natural inclination to gravitate towards the more lucrative parts of the territory and to avoid the less attractive areas. SST points out rightly that in today's economic climate companies grow, move in, move out and thus change the sales potential of an area. SST recommends a technique whereby 'zones' are created according to the status of prospects therein. The classification of zones might be:

A zone: should close business in 90 days

B zone: should close business in six months

C zone: should close business this financial year

D zone: potential business with some interest

E zone: potential business with no interest so far

F zone: no apparent potential for business

The zone values determine the number of days each period which the salesman will allocate to prospecting and follow-up calling. At the end of a call the prospect organisation will be reclassified if necessary and reallocated to a higher or lower zone.

7.2.2 Sources of Information

As will be discussed in Section 7.5, the maintenance of comprehensive records is an essential part of *operating* a territory. Access to information is also vital to the planning process. Thus the professional salesman will use a variety of directories and information databases to build the necessary records which will help provide a realistic assessment of territory sales potential. Sometimes the marketing services departments of IT supplier companies will keep sets of essential directories at head office and provide access to them. In some cases the information will be compiled into a marketing database with on-line access to all branch offices. Should information not be available in house, most directories can be seen in the commercial/business sections of the larger public libraries. The following is a selection of some widely read directories (see Appendix 4).

Key British Enterprises

Municipal Year Book and Public Services Directory

Trade Associations and Professional Bodies of the UK

Kompass

Europe's 10,000 Largest Companies

Britain's Privately Owned Companies (The Top 2000 Survey)

The City Directory

Directory of European Associations

Computer Users' Year Book

National Computer Index (NCI)

Who's Who in Computing

Market Location

7.3 TIME MANAGEMENT

7.3.1 Time Expenditure

A saleman's time is spent on a wide range of activities, most being essential to the job, but in the main *non-revenue earning*. These activities include:

— Revenue earning:	Making sales visits
	Making sales presentations
— Non-revenue earning:	Travelling
	Reading: literature, memoranda, reports and correspondence
	Writing: reports, letters, memoranda, proposals
	Meetings: with support staff and management
	Attending: exhibitions, trade shows, sales conventions, progress meetings
	Planning: appointments, hotel rooms

Waiting

Training

The non-revenue earning activities can quite easily expend 30 hours per week.

7.3.2 Using Time Effectively

Clearly selling is not a 'nine-to-five' job. Professional salesmen work much longer than the standard 38 hours per week. But, like the owner of the small business the successful salesman uses these hours effectively. This involves using as much *prime selling time* as possible in negotiating and closing business. Prime selling time means those specific hours in which the salesman can realistically meet with clients, namely:

09.30–12.30

14.00–16.30

The 'expenditure' of these hours on non-revenue earning activities should be avoided whenever possible.

7.3.3 Setting Priorities

Effective use of one's time also involves the setting of priorities. The following parameters should be applied:

- problem account requiring urgent attention;
- size and profitability of customer account;
- estimated revenue from the sale;
- probability factor (of getting the order);
- level of sales and support involvement;
- company directive;
- complacency factor.

Problem account is top of the list because no salesman can afford to have a single dissatisfied customer. The professional knows only too well how fast 'bad news' travels in a territory.

Complacency refers to the need to visit the apparently satisfied 'quiet' customer. He or she may be having meetings with the competition anxious to 'move in'.

A variety of tools are available to help the salesman rank his prospects. Specialist IT sales trainers such as Strategic Sales Training Ltd (SST) include these techniques in their sales training workshops. SST makes the point however that tools cannot substitute for the salesman's judgement. They are intended to help him/her to become a *businessman*.

7.4 TRAINING

As was mentioned in Section 6.1.1, training is a continuous process. It does not stop at one's appointment to a territory.

7.4.1 Product Update

All products change by enhancement or replacement. The addition of new features may require only a brief reference to the latest issue of a technical manual. If it is of greater significance, training may be provided at regional/branch progress meetings or at sales conferences. New product releases will involve attendance on company courses or at briefings organised by sales support personnel.

7.4.2 Technology Updates

Changes in this dynamic technology are reported regularly in the technical press and often disseminated by the information departments of IT suppliers. Sometimes they become the subjects of symposia, seminars or conferences arranged by IT specialist organisations. Regular advertisements for such events are included in the technical journals and those of professional societies. The IT salesman should read such papers.

7.4.3 Mainstream Systems Environments

Again the products and other issues such as compatibility, change from time to time. Information on such matters is normally available through the sales literature of major suppliers and particularly via their consultant liaison services. Provided that the company's products do not compete head on with the mainstream manufacturers' offerings but enhance their users' installations, regular newsletters are generally obtainable. In any event, major new releases and policy changes are reported in the technical magazines to which free circulation is normally given.

7.4.4 Sales Training

The territory salesperson in IT can be likened to an airline captain. Both are experienced professionals but require regular 'check-ups'. Irrespective of the flying hours clocked in a particular type of aircraft, all airline pilots are subjected to six-monthly flying checks under the supervision of a training captain. Even the top professional golfers find that on occasions a fault develops in a normally reliable swing. A session with an experienced teacher will usually suffice to iron out the fault and thus return the player to the winner's rostrum.

Just as the training captain tests the pilot's reaction to an emergency situation so the sales manager or sales training manager tests the ability of the salesman to handle objections, close business and so on. Role playing exercises at progress meetings, conventions or formal sales training courses are never popular but the professional salesperson knows that the objective is to maintain a high standard of salesmanship. It is better to make mistakes in front of one's colleagues than in a client's office.

7.5 TERRITORY RECORDS

7.5.1 Essential Records

Administrative tasks, form filling and the submission of timely reports are an anathema to most salespeople. Nonetheless the maintenance of concise and quickly accessible records is essential to successful selling. Thus the services of a competent and understanding branch secretary are an essential part of the selling team. The branch secretary will probably handle the administration and files of several salespeople, ensuring that appointments are kept, diaries are updated, enquiries are handled, letters written, and company reports are submitted on time.

Essential territory records comprise:

— customer file;

— prospective customer file;

— internal correspondence file;

— sales reports.

7.5.2 Customer File

Sequence: Alpha/chronological

A single four-drawer cabinet with a provision for hanging files vertically will suffice for most needs. A folder may then be used for each customer and filed alphabetically. Attached to the front of each folder should be a customer record sheet giving the following minimum information:

— customer name and address;

— telephone number;

— name(s) and title(s) of main contact;

— product usage;

— computer installation data: hardware, peripherals, communications;

— software data: operating system, main languages, system software;

— type of business (SIC code);

— computer applications: main areas;

— company T/O;

— no of employees;

— no of IT staff.

Copies of *all* correspondence, records of meetings and internal memoranda relevant to the customer should be kept in the folder, ideally in chronological order with the most recent document at the front. The folder can thus be removed from the file and used by the salesman as an *aide-mémoire* at meetings or during telephone communications.

7.5.3 Prospective Customer File

Sequence: Alpha/chronological

This should be maintained in a manner similar to that exercised for the customer file. In starting to compile a prospective customer file from scratch, much information can be obtained from the sources discussed in Section 7.2.2 and the professional salesman will be familiar with the range of directories available through the company's marketing services department (Appendix 4).

7.5.4 Internal Correspondence File

Provision should be made for:

- management/administration notices;
- product data/marketing information;
- minutes of branch/regional progress meetings;
- correspondence with individuals;
- sales reports.

7.5.5 Sales Reports

Requirements will vary between companies, but generally a territory salesman will submit the following each period end (four weekly):

- *Current prospects list*

  A dynamic listing of those companies deemed prospects for sales, with an indication of sales value, probability of closure and estimated order date (Figure 7.2).

- *Forecast income statement*

  A forecast for the year of income by product (Figures 7.3a and b) and supported by papers justifying the forecast.

- *Quarterly review statement*

  An intermediate forecast at the end of periods 4, 7, 10 and 13 with supporting notes justifying the forecast and explaining variances for 'this' quarter (Figures 7.4a and b).

- *Visit report*

  Provides a list of visits made in both planned (Section 7.2.1) and unplanned (Figure 7.5) mode.

- *Local presentations*

  A list of attendees at locally organised functions (Figure 7.6).

7.5.6 Daily Letter File

Finally, as a long stop in case outgoing correspondence should go astray, it is sensible to maintain a daily letter file. All correspondence and memoranda sent by the salesman should be copied to this file and held in chronological order.

Salesman ....

Prospect list no ....

Territory ....

Prospect name	Product	Source	Next action	Potential for sales		
				Probability (%)	Value	Date

Figure 7.2   Current Prospect List

Salesman.................

Territory.................

Period no.................

Product/service	A Orders not invoiced	B Invoiced	A+B Secure	C Qualified prospects	A+B+C Forecast	Target (year)	Variance	+/-
Total new business								

c/f

Figure 7.3a   Forecast Income Statement (New Business)

Salesman ....
Territory ....
Period no ....

Product/service	A Orders not invoiced	B Invoiced	A+B Secure	C Qualified prospects	A+B+C Forecast	Target (year)	Variance +/−
Total renewals							
Total new business							
Total all business							

b/f

Figure 7.3b   Forecast Income Statement (Renewals)

Salesman .... Territory ....
Quarter no. ....

Product/service	This quarter				Next quarter				Year end			
	Actual	Forecast	Variance	+/–	Forecast	Target	Variance	+/–	Forecast	Target	Variance	+/–
Total new business												

c/f

Figure 7.4a   Quarterly Review Statement (New Business)

Salesman .... Territory ....
Quarter no. ....

Product/service	This quarter				Next quarter				Year end			
	Actual	Forecast	Variance	+/-	Forecast	Target	Variance	+/-	Forecast	Target	Variance	+/-
Total renewals												
Total new business												
Total all business												
Controllable expenses												
Travel/subsistence												
Other external												
Total expenses												

b/f

Figure 7.4b　Quarterly Review Statement (Renewals)

Sales visits	Period		Cumulative	
	Actual	Targeted	Actual	Targeted
Scheduled				
Unscheduled				
Total				

Salesman............................

Territory.............................

Period no............................

Company name	Reason for visit	Follow-up action

Figure 7.5   Visit Report

Branch..............................   Period..............................

Territory ....

Delegate	Company	Product interest	Follow-up action

Figure 7.6   Local Presentations

In the event that word processing equipment is used at the branch and all correspondence held on disk, the simple hard copy daily letter file is still a boon and can be browsed through each month just to check that all actions 'promised' have in fact been undertaken.

7.6 SALES AIDS

Before undertaking a sales visit, the IT salesperson should ensure that the following product and sales aids are available:

— Documentation:	Product brochures
	Product manuals
— Sales aids:	Demonstration scripts
	Prospect qualification checklist
	Objection handling notes
	Case histories
— Other:	Price list
	Contract forms
	Acceptance documents
	Customer/prospect folder

Provision of such data is normally made through marketing services.

7.7 THE SELLING PROCESS

7.7.1 Continuity

It is important to appreciate that operating a sales territory, like running a business, is a continuous process. It does not begin and end with the fiscal year. However, the *performance* of the territory salesman is measured throughout each financial year and the professional must come to terms with this fact.

Consider Table 7.2: two salesmen with independent territories but each having identical sales quotas. Over a three-year period, Salesman A has achieved 108% performance against the target but has missed earning the bonus incentive payment on five occasions including the annual bonus in

Year	Cumulative sales target (£K)	Salesman A			Salesman B		
		Cumulative sales (£K)	Performance (%)	Bonus earned (Yes/No)	Cumulative sales (£K)	Performance (%)	Bonus earned (Yes/No)
1							
Q1	150.0	180.0	120	Yes	160.0	107	Yes
Q2	300.0	354.0	118	Yes	320.0	107	Yes
Q3	450.0	427.5	95	No	440.0	98	No
Q4	600.0	636.0	106	Yes	608.0	101	Yes
Year 1 bonus				Yes			Yes
2							
Q1	165.0	148.5	90	No	170.0	103	Yes
Q2	330.0	330.0	100	Yes	350.0	106	Yes
Q3	495.0	524.7	106	Yes	505.0	102	Yes
Q4	660.0	640.2	97	No	675.0	102	Yes
Year 2 bonus				No			Yes
3							
Q1	182.0	254.8	140	Yes	202.0	111	Yes
Q2	364.0	371.3	102	Yes	380.0	104	Yes
Q3	546.0	524.2	96	No	530.0	97	No
Q4	728.0	873.6	120	Yes	760.0	104	Yes
Year 3 bonus				Yes			Yes
Total	1988	2149.8	108		2043.0	103	

Table 7.2   Example Comparative Performance Over 3 Years

year 2. Salesman B has achieved a lower overall performance of 103% but has missed the bonus only twice.

Given that their employer does not pay commission on sales value, it is likely that B's earnings over the three years will be substantially higher than A's.

Some of the factors contributing to A's dilemma may be outside his/her control. These are facts of life and A must have the courage to accept them. However it is probable that B is the better organised and the more professional salesman of the two. B will be ever conscious that to hit targets at the right time requires him/her to maintain a *continuous and adequate prospect list*. As prospects are converted into the orders the list must be topped up with new prospects – potential customers which have been identified and *qualified*.

7.7.2 Steps to a Sale

When Dougal Haston and Don Whillans finally stood on the top of Annapurna, having negotiated the formidable south face route, their achievement was the culmination of expedition research, meticulous planning, organisation, equipment design and logistics, together with the application of their accumulated knowledge, mountaineering techniques and strength of character. Without the support of base camp, the medical officer, sherpas, route finders capable of fixing ropes and establishing camps, it is unlikely that the final summit assault would have been mounted, let alone achieved by these exceptional men.

Less dramatically the IT salesman will have:

– researched the territory and established its potential;

– planned a sales campaign;

– understood the importance of time;

– acquired the necessary level of knowledge and expertise;

– equipped himself/herself with records and sales aids.

Like the mountaineer, the salesman is ready to scale the peak.

Selling a product or service comprises six steps:

– approach;

– prove the need;

– show credibility;

– describe the product;

– quantify the benefits;

– close the sale.

These essential steps are carried out as part of the salesman–customer dialogue: in telephone conversations, during visits, at product demonstrations, in written proposals, or during formal presentations.

7.7.3 Approach

Pre-prospecting

Before any approach call is made some planning and pre-prospecting should have taken place, using directories and territory records. Apart from helping to establish the possible scope for doing business, such research will provide the salesman with some *credibility* in the eyes of the prospect. The zoning and territory classification techniques referred to in Section 7.2.1 may well have been applied to this task.

At this stage the prospect will not have been *qualified,* unless the approach has come from the prospect in the nature of an enquiry or as a response to some promotional event such as an exhibition or mail-shot. Even in these latter cases the level of qualification is likely to be low, albeit the prospect has expressed an interest.

Using the Telephone

Many salespeople use the telephone to approach an organisation for the first time, rather than make a cold canvas call. There is much to be gained by this approach:

 — Many contacts can be made in a relatively short time.

 — Firm appointments can be fixed in a professional manner. A cold call may offend the prospect by assuming that he/she has time to spare, which is rarely true.

 — Much information can be gleaned concerning the organisation itself, the best contact and possibly the *needs* of both organisation and contact.

Of course the telephone cannot replace the physical call. It is devoid of all visual aids, person-to-person contact, facial expressions, voice inflexion and all the other *signs* which are present in a face-to-face situation. Furthermore it is easier for a potential client to say 'no' over the telephone.

In summary the telephone can be used to great effect in 'breaking the ice', obtaining information and fixing firm appointments.

7.7.4 Proving the Need

*Do not buy what you want, but what you need; what you do not
need is dear at a farthing.*

— Cato 234–149 BC

Some salespeople are prone to exaggeration especially in their determination of *prospects*. They provide their sales managers with impressive-looking prospect lists and months later the same names are still present — they have not been converted into *users*. If a 'prospect' is unlikely to place an order within six months or if the probability of closure is less than 75% then it should not appear on the prospect list but be regarded as a lower priority case with a *possibility* of development over a longer period.

Proving the need for one's product is concerned with *prospect qualification* and failure to meet any of the qualification criteria will probably result in losing the order. During meetings with the potential client, the professional salesman should determine the following:

Need

    — What are the shortcomings of the existing system?

    — What are the effects of such shortcomings on the company?

    — How do these shortcomings *concern* the decision maker?

    — How can we justify our solution in quantifiable terms?

Decision Maker

— Who will make the decision to proceed?

    • One person?

    • A board?

— If a board, who will make the recommendation?

— How successful has he/she been in previous recommendations?

— Who are likely to *influence* the decision?

    • Outside consultants?

    • Friends in business?

    • Users?

    • Technical staff?

- Who will place the order?
  - The decision maker?
  - The buyer?
  - The contracts manager?

Budget

- Is there a specific IT budget?
- Is this transaction additional to the annual replacement budget?
- What is its value?
- When does the budget period expire?

Timescale

- When will the decision be taken?
- Will it be dependent on a trial or benchmark test?
- If so, for what period of time?
- How will the order be placed once the decision to proceed is taken?

Cost of Sale

- Will *we* be involved in a lengthy and costly sales exercise?
- Will it involve setting up:
  - Benchmark tests?
  - Site visits?
  - Trials?
  - Systems investigation?

Competition

- Who else is competing for the business?
- Are they already established in the prospect's company?
- Can we offer a different and better solution?

Compatibility

- Do we need to interface with another supplier's products?
- What minimum configuration of such systems does our product require?

Exclusiveness

- Can we demonstrate a unique ability to meet this potential customer's needs?
- Is our product exclusive?

Further Business

- Is there scope for further applications?

For those wishing to study this important subject further it is exhaustively dealt with in *Selling Professional Services* (Davis, 1984) and in the video case study *The Importance of Qualification* produced by Strategic Sales Training Ltd.

7.7.5 Showing Credibility

In forging a sound relationship with a prospective customer, it is essential that the IT salesman should create a high degree of confidence in his company, its products, and in himself.

Corporate Image

All progressive IT companies are conscious of their corporate identity and do much to project their ideal image amongst their various publics. Publics can be the government, the customers, the industry, the press or even the general public. The corporate image is reflected *inter alia* in correspondence, stationery design, publicity material, product packaging, company reports, articles and advertising. When dealing with prospective customers the salesman should use such material and thus demonstrate his company's reputation, stability and high emphasis on customer satisfaction.

Product Image

In projecting product credibility the salesman should lean heavily on pedigree and reference sales. Good product brochures include a paragraph on the company's long experience in research and development. This helps convince the client that the product has anticipated and solved most of the problems likely to be encountered by the user. 'Use your users' is an old selling maxim and never fails to impress that the product is field proven.

Personal Credibility

Salesmen should avoid 'talking down' to a customer, arguing, using jargon and 'name dropping'. Personal credibility is best achieved through sympathetic listening, understanding the client's needs and describing a solution in a language the client can understand.

7.7.6 Describing the Product

The portfolios of today's IT salespeople are many and varied, ranging from a simple software product to computer systems involving hardware, software and communications facilities. In describing a product (or service, or solution) the salesman should keep to a sequence. This ensures that whenever the presentation is interrupted, he/she can return to the point and thus cover all the essential features and benefits of the product. The description of a computer system designed for fault-tolerant transaction processing might include:

- a product overview;
- an outline of the 'family' architecture;
- product features such as:
  - processor,
  - systems software,
  - communications hardware,
  - communications software,
  - peripherals,
  - support facilities.

The description of the product should be related to both customer needs and benefits.

In the example in Tables 7.3a and b, the customer (company) has five basic needs but the recommender has two further (personal) concerns. The presentation would be geared as shown.

Customer need	Product benefits	Product features
1 Must be capable of processing over 100 transactions per sec	Can produces 4 times the processing power of current system in excess of 150 tps	Advanced 32-bit VLSI chip technology. Faster memory read access of 120 ns
2 Must have high growth potential	Can be added to incrementally to 8 times basic processing power	Modular processor of 8 MB duplex memory and 150 MB disk storage
3 Must combine with present (Mark 1) system without re-programming	Full software compatibility	Compatible operating system
4 Must link with corporate network using SNA and X.25 protocols	Capable of full range of networking, device emulation and technical connectivity	ASCII terminal and PC connectivity. Guaranteed functions with SNA and CCITT X.25, X.29 standards
5 Must be very reliable	Capable of non-stop computing	Hardware fault tolerance built in. Automatic monitoring of its own performance. Duplicate processor

Table 7.3a   Example Presentation According to Customer Needs

Concerns	Benefits	Features
1 Fear of making wrong decision	Best selling system on the market	Large company with sound reputation
2 Wish to raise personal status	Chosen by top 'blue chip' companies	Favoured by companies in this industry

Table 7.3b   Example Presentation According to Customer Concerns

7.7.7 Quantifying the Benefits

Relating to Needs and Concerns

A benefit is something of value – value to an organisation and to the individual. When 'proving the need' the salesman will have asked a number of questions aimed at securing information on the real needs of the organisation and securing the involvement of his contact. Once the corporate needs of the prospective customer have been determined and a solution drafted, it then becomes necessary to *relate* the benefits of the solution to the needs. But the benefits must also relate to the *concerns* of the individual with whom the salesman is negotiating – this individual may be the decision maker or recommender.

The individual is personally motivated by:

- Safety: Concern for the security of his/her job
- Performance: Concern that he/she is satisfying end-users
- Appearance: Concern that the product looks good to users
- Comfort: Concern that he/she has made the right decision
- Economy: Concern that the change is economically viable
- Durability: Concern for long-term safety

Money Terms

Benefits are frequently a *saving* of money, time and effort. However the astute salesman will seek further, more positive benefits. He/she will be aware that the client is not just increasing profits by reducing costs. Further needs will include better servicing of their customers and increased liquidity to invest in both customer servicing and research and development. Both will help increase market share and sales revenues.

An ability to understand financial statements is an essential requirement of an IT salesman. It can be used to support and quantify the benefits of his/her proposal. At the 'proving the need' stage the salesman should seek a viewing of the client's accounts for the current and previous years. It will reveal much about the organisation such as:

- the effect of this year's modest increase in turnover on profit;
- the effect of new plant investment on cost of sales;

- the effect of an increase in work-in-progress and finished goods stocks on the company's cash flow;

- the effect of an increase in sales and administration overheads on the company's profit.

Such information could prompt further questions:

- Is the company turnover being inhibited by over lengthy manufacturing lead times?

- If so would a vastly improved production scheduling system be desirable?

- Would better and more timely information help optimise stock levels without jeopardising customer service?

- If so an improved cash flow could help finance growth in other areas.

Quantified benefits are likely to secure a positive response from the prospect and the salesman should obtain *agreement* whenever possible and confirm the fact in his/her formal proposal (see Section 7.8.4).

7.7.8 Closing the Sale

Closing the business is the culmination of all the carefully prepared and executed steps in the selling cycle. This crunch step is the salesman's *raison d'être*.

Fearing the Close

Many otherwise excellent salespeople fear the close. To begin with, it is not as easy to prepare as, for example, a product demonstration. The real fear however is that of *rejection*. The successful salesman will overcome this fear by learning how to:

- recognise and react to *buying signals;*

- handle sales *resistances;*

- understand the value of *'no';*

- appply a variety of well-proven *closing techniques.*

He/she will also appreciate the qualification: closing relationship. The better qualified the prospect the greater the likelihood of closure! The professional salesman will have developed a closing instinct by applying a *trial* close whenever the opportunity presents itself during any stage in the selling cycle.

Buying Signals

Marketing theory suggests that a buyer will move through six stages:

— *Awareness*

The need is felt: the buyer is aware of products that can help.

— *Knowledge*

The fact-finding stage.

— *Liking*

Features of particular products have an appeal.

— *Conviction*

Decision to go ahead but iron out detail.

— *Purchase*

Formal contract.

Buying signals will reflect these stages during sales meetings and in correspondence. They often take the form of questions such as:

— Can your product be leased over five years?

— How soon can you deliver?

— Can you arrange a free trial?

— How fast is your maintenance service?

— Can you demonstrate the product to our full board?

— Would you be a party to an escrow agreement?

The salesperson should react positively to these signals, taking care to answer all questions fully and generating a 'when' rather than 'if' dialogue with the client.

Handling Sales Resistances

There are eight basic reasons why a prospective customer says 'no'.

Change

'No problems with present system.'
'Change will be a problem.'

In this example, the salesman should reduce the impression of change by concentrating on evolution (not revolution); emphasising the risks in the present system; offering support and participation in problem solving; giving examples of other organisations which have benefited from change.

Past Experience

'We had difficulty with a similar product.'

Here the salesman should establish the differences between the previous situation and the present offer but at the same time show an understanding of the client's feelings.

Saturation

'We've got enough.'

Again the salesman should emphasise the differences between his/her offer and the existing products and encourage the prospect to consider long-term planning.

Authority

'It's not my decision.'

The salesman should have already ensured that he/she is in negotiation with the decision maker or recommender. This can be difficult since people are often reluctant to concede this lack of authority at the early stages. The salesman must discover the distribution of authority in the client organisation and establish multilateral and multilevel contacts without causing offence to his contact.

Time

'Not at the moment.'

The salesman should try to gain something by a 'supposing the time were right, would our proposal be acceptable' line of approach, finding out when the situation might change and suggesting an objective for the next visit.

Influence

'I'll make up my own mind.'

Although high pressure selling might succeed in the short term, it has no place in the IT industry.

The salesman should demonstrate empathy with the customer by asking questions. Although the salesman should adopt a positive attitude, in no circumstances should he/she argue with the customer. There is no point in winning an argument but losing the sale.

Unsuitable

'Not really what we want.'

This difference between the offer and the customer's perception of the product to help meet his needs often occurs at the initial stage of a sale. The salesman should be prepared for this first refusal and concentrate on the idea rather than the product itself.

Price

'Can't afford it.'

It is always easy to assume that price is the major factor in the purchase decision. By concentrating on selling value and benefits the salesman will make price a far less important issue.

The Value of 'No'

The professional salesman will welcome objections since people who do not ask – do not buy! 'No' allows the salesman to discuss the objection and equate it. Therefore 'no' is undoubtedly better than 'don't know'.

Closing Techniques

The good salesman will *build* his close throughout the sales cycle by obtaining agreement on his/her individual proposals as they occur, regularly summarising these acceptances, and obtaining decisions on major issues. All will lead to the *final* closing of the business. Examples of formal closing methods include:

Summary Close

The main points of the proposal are repeated, together with the actions now required of the prospect. The salesman asks the prospect to agree and sign a formal order.

Final Objection Close

If the prospect raises a further issue, the salesman should aim to turn it into a *final* objection, asking the prospect: 'If we can solve this problem, will you sign?'.

Secondary Question Close

In this example, the salesman assumes that the prospect has made the decision to buy. The question will be concerned with the formalities involved in concluding the business.

Reference Close

This involves showing the prospect how another company had decided to purchase the product and how successful that decision had been.

There are many more closing techniques, which can be found in textbooks and sales training courses. Generally it pays to ask questions which demand a 'yes' answer. The more points accepted by the prospect the easier it is to overcome objections.

7.8 SALES ACTIVITIES

The professional salesman will apply all the techniques of selling – approach, proving the need, creating confidence, describing the product, quantifying the benefits and closing the business – during:

- sales calls;

- surveys;

- demonstrations;

- presentations.

Good practice should be applied to all such activities.

7.8.1 The Sales Call

A good sales call will include:

- thanking the receptionist;

- seeing the right person;

- setting call objectives;

- making an impact in the first minute;

- outlining the scope of one's products;
- using reference sales;
- keeping the door open for follow-up activity.

7.8.2 The Survey

A systems survey is an opportunity to gain all the essential information for the subsequent proposal. The salesman should:

- make use of a standard questionnaire;
- arrange appointments through the principal contact;
- ensure that the activity does not inconvenience staff;
- set people at ease;
- undertake the survey logically;
- pay close attention to volumes and shortcomings;
- appreciate the importance of influencers.

7.8.3 The Demonstration

This is the opportunity to show the capability of the product, its ease of operation and its relevance to the customer's requirements. Failure can mean starting all over again, especially if credibility has been lost. It can even mean the end of the line with this particular prospect. The following should be considered:

- pre-demonstration rehearsal with briefing of operator and support staff;
- most suitable venue;
- room preparation;
- equipment check;
- briefing of delegates, introducing participants and showing what demonstration will cover;
- sequential showing of essential features;
- salesman to stand behind the terminal;

- answering objections as they occur and returning to the point left in the sequence.

7.8.4 Presentation of Proposal

We'll make him an offer he can't refuse.

— Marlon Brando (*The Godfather*)

The Proposal

The written proposal is the culmination of all the selling activities which have taken place. In itself it will *not* achieve the sale and it is important to appreciate that *all* points made in the report should have been *agreed* before writing. In other words it is a formal confirmation of agreement with the decision maker or recommender.

The proposal should contain:

- a management summary and request to proceed;

- a contents list;

- extent and conclusions of survey;

- summary of scope of existing system;

- scope of proposed system;

- schedule of benefits;

- schedule of proposed equipment and services;

- costs and savings;

- implementation programme;

- contract or licence forms.

The Presentation

Generally the presentation of the proposal will be done formally. The proposal should *not* be mailed to the prospect.

Great care should be taken in the following:

- arrange a time which will allow sufficient scope for preparation, delivery and questions/answers;

- check the room size and the most appropriate visual aids;
- brief all support staff;
- do not circulate copies of the proposal before the presentation;
- use a presentation sequence which follows that in the written proposal;
- if overhead transparencies are used, have them made professionally;
- if a slide projector is used, note the number of each slide and where it appears in the presentation sequence;
- have a blank flip chart handy to provide amplification;
- rehearse the presentation and become familiar with the sequence;
- use *cue cards* and do *not* read;
- avoid jargon.

At the end of the presentation:

- circulate copies of the proposal;
- ask for authority to proceed.

Part 3

Career Progression

Ambition should be made of sterner stuff.

— William Shakespeare

8 Promotion Path

8.1 OVERVIEW

For reasons of ability, opportunity or inclination relatively few IT salespeople will progress beyond operating a sales territory. The role of *managing* is far removed from that of *selling* and requires a variety of further skills which not all salesmen will possess, nor have the potential to develop. Many highly successful salesmen have failed in sales management through an inability to demonstrate leadership qualities. Such situations have had unfortunate consequences for both the company and the individual.

Thus management selection is a difficult process which looks far beyond an ability to close business and retain clients. When combined with the ratio of managers to salesmen it will be obvious that only a few will attain senior management status. For many salespeople this will not matter one jot! They will gain maximum satisfaction from running a sales territory and hitting sales targets. Their financial rewards will be high, frequently exceeding those of line management and they will enjoy relatively high security. In times of recession the good salesmen are very secure indeed, in keeping the company alive with a larger share of a diminishing market. In times of plenty, they are the instrument of growth. However, the ambitious ones will be motivated to achieve self-fulfilment by reaching the top echelons of the company. Such IT salespeople will already possess some understanding of:

— organisational theory and behaviour;

— change;

— motivation;

— achieving objectives.

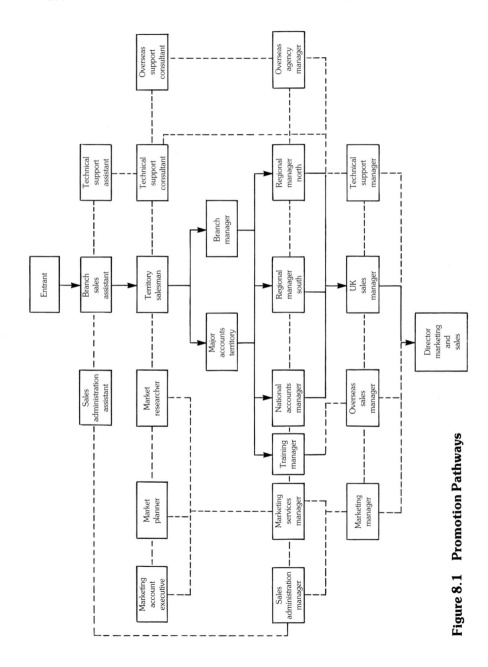

Figure 8.1   Promotion Pathways

For them a variety of routes (Figure 8.1) exist. The most obvious, as indicated by the unbroken lines, are through major accounts or branch management, national accounts or regional sales management, into national sales management and possibly the directorship of marketing and sales.

One problem with the *direct* route is that the candidate for subsequent promotion to top management is confining all his/her experience to the selling process. Therefore in career terms, it could be valuable to seek transfers into other sections of the marketing group as indicated by the horizontal broken lines in the figure. The aspirant would thus gain a more rounded experience of the marketing process. Not only would such variety improve the individual but such exchanges would bring a greater degree of field knowledge to the various marketing departments.

8.2 THE NATURE OF MANAGEMENT

8.2.1 Different Skills

Beyond the level of territory sales operation, the contender for higher management now enters a whole new ball park. Up to this stage it is unlikely that he/she will have had the responsibility of managing people. Quite apart from understanding the mechanics of the company's management structure and policies, the candidate chosen for promotion will need to learn much about the role of the manager, the nature of leadership, the related behavioural theory, organisational theory, and the art of negotiation. This requires him/her to wear a number of hats to suit the many different situations doubtless to be faced.

8.2.2 The Role of the Manager

Definition

Professional management is a major discipline now very well taught in the business schools and management faculties of our universities and polytechnics. Many excellent books have also been published on the subject and some are mentioned in the bibliography. Thus anything but a glimpse of some of the more important aspects of management is beyond the scope of this book.

Management can be defined as the process of getting things done through other people.

Some might take a step back and define management as *deciding what needs to be done and getting somebody else to do it.*

In order to fulfil this role the manager must therefore:

- lead;

- motivate;

- delegate;

- plan;

- monitor;

- control;

- negotiate;

- train;

- develop;

- direct;

- discipline;

- organise;

- take responsibility for achieving objectives.

Leadership

It is important for a manager to distinguish between management and leadership.

Leadership is a part of the manager's role and may be defined as the process of influencing people to direct their activity to achieve particular objectives.

Leadership is the subject of much research by the behavioural scientist. Some suggest that a leader's influence derives from two sources – the *legitimate authority* vested in the job and the *compliance* of the subordinates. To secure this latter co-operation the leader will need to display competence, support through his/her influence with top management, and an ability to reward. Exceptional leaders have a charismatic quality which subordinates will wish to emulate.

Group Needs

In managing a group the leader must satisfy three classes of needs (Figure 8.2).

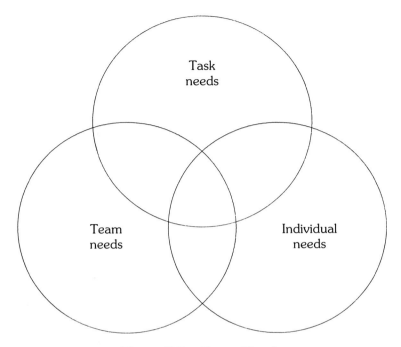

Figure 8.2   Group Needs

Task Needs

To meet these needs the manager will allocate responsibility for tasks, battle for resources, define clearly the tasks of each member of the group, set up controls, and through the feedback of results, modify tasks to ensure that they are still achievable.

Team Needs

In order to satisfy the needs of the team, the manager will ensure that all members know where they fit in, let them see the plan progressing, show them how they are performing, resolve group conflicts, defend the group, and discipline the group.

Individual Needs

The leader, whether a branch, regional or national sales manager, will be aware that all individuals have needs which Maslow (1954) postulated were five in number and in ascending order:

Need	Example
1 Physiological	Food and shelter
2 Safety	Security and stability
3 Social	Social interaction
4 Esteem	Recognition
5 Self-actualisation	Realising one's potential

Clearly leadership is a complex skill.

Other Relevant Skills

As suggested earlier, the new manager will need to acquire and develop a number of further skills in undertaking the tasks required by the job. Such management and leadership skills are sometimes provided by progressive IT companies as part of a management training and learning programme. These programmes are often carried out in conjunction with business schools, polytechnics or management consultancies. The preliminary stages of such courses will include essential topics such as:

Delegation

By giving people *responsibility* for what they already do, delegation can be a first-class motivator.

Control

The risk associated with delegation is that of losing control. It is important that such authority as is given be *monitored* at agreed times.

Communication

This art of being *understood* is helped by understanding the needs of one's 'audience' and by using feedback.

Discipline

This difficult aspect of management is concerned with speaking *on behalf of* the company. In censuring an individual, the manager must demonstrate that the boss, not he himself, is speaking. That *we* (the company and the boss) are not satisfied with a given situation.

There are many further skills which the manager will acquire and develop over time. Those outlined earlier should provide a sample of some of the skills which will need to be applied by branch, regional and sales managers of IT companies.

8.3 LEVELS OF IT SALES MANAGEMENT

8.3.1 Direct Route

In the remainder of this chapter we will consider the role and responsibilities of the various levels of sales management leading to that of marketing director. For simplicity a direct route has been chosen:

— major accounts territory management;

— branch sales management;

— regional sales management;

— national sales management;

— director of marketing.

Most of the competition for the first four levels will come from *within* the salesforce or from external IT salespeople. Competition for the final level will derive from *all* managers in the marketing group, including the sales manager, and from external sources. It is for the company to decide whether a salesman might be groomed for senior marketing management by secondment or promotion into other parts of the marketing operation. Should the territory salesperson believe that he/she could benefit from that route then the matter should be raised at the annual appraisal. If such openings are not forthcoming then the candidate might wish to seek them elsewhere.

8.3.2 Company Model

To illustrate the nature of the levels of sales management, we will use as a model an imaginary IT company, ABC Products Ltd. ABC Products Ltd (Figure 8.3; Tables 8.1–8.3) is an expanding IT software and consultancy company with a sound reputation for providing software engineering tools. The anticipated turnover in the forthcoming year is in excess of £30 million, including £10 million overseas business earned through its European agencies.

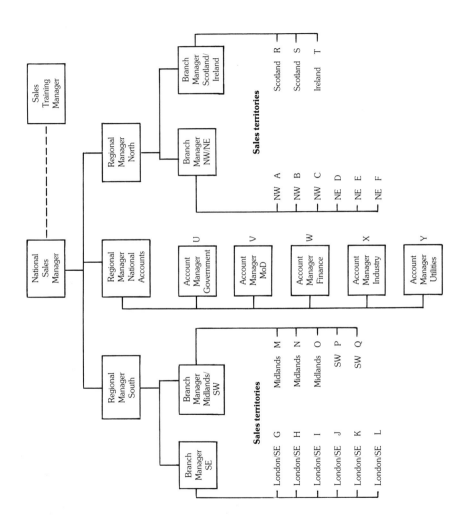

Figure 8.3   Company Model 1: UK Sales Organisation

Territory	Product A				Product B				Pr. C
	New licence	New maintenance	Licence renewals	Maintenance renewals	New licence	New maintenance	Licence renewals	Maintenance renewals	New sales
A NW	9	9	4	30	10	10	0	15	11
B NW	9	9	3	28	10	10	0	14	11
C NW	9	9	4	26	10	10	0	13	11
D NE	9	9	4	35	10	10	0	6	11
E NE	9	9	4	25	10	10	0	12	11
F NE	9	9	4	22	10	10	0	11	11
G L/SE	9	9	4	40	10	10	0	20	11
H L/SE	9	9	4	34	10	10	0	17	11
I L/SE	9	9	4	31	10	10	0	15	11
J L/SE	9	9	4	37	10	10	0	18	11
K L/SE	9	9	4	39	10	10	0	20	11
L L/SE	9	9	4	30	10	10	0	15	11
M Midlands	9	9	3	31	10	10	0	15	11
N Midlands	9	9	3	32	10	10	0	16	11
O Midlands	9	9	3	32	10	10	0	16	11
P SW	6	6	2	10	7	7	0	5	7
Q SW	6	6	2	8	7	7	0	4	7
R Scotland	5	5	2	12	5	5	0	6	6
S Scotland	5	5	2	9	5	5	0	4	6
T Ireland	5	5	2	10	6	6	0	5	6
U Government	11	11	8	42	16	16	0	21	16
V MoD	8	8	5	20	9	9	0	10	10
W Finance	12	12	8	94	18	18	0	49	19
X Industry	11	11	5	26	11	11	0	13	26
Y Utilities	11	11	8	50	16	16	0	25	18
Total units	215	215	100	750	250	250	0	375	286
Value £K	6450	645	3000	2250	2500	250	0	375	4576

**Table 8.1   Company Model 2: UK Sales Target Units
by Territory**

| Territory | New business | | | Renewals business | | | Sales target (£K) |
	Product sales	Maintenance	Total	Licence renewals	Maintenance renewals	Total	
A	546	37	583	120	105	225	808
B	546	37	583	90	98	188	771
C	546	37	583	120	91	211	794
D	546	37	583	120	112	232	815
E	546	37	583	120	87	207	790
F	546	37	583	120	77	197	780
G	546	37	583	120	140	260	843
H	546	37	583	120	119	239	822
I	546	37	583	120	108	228	811
J	546	37	583	120	129	249	832
K	546	37	583	120	137	257	840
L	546	37	583	120	105	225	808
M	546	37	583	90	108	198	781
N	546	37	583	90	112	202	785
O	546	37	583	90	112	202	785
P	362	25	387	60	35	95	482
Q	362	25	387	60	28	88	475
R	296	20	316	60	42	102	418
S	296	20	316	60	31	91	407
T	306	21	327	60	35	95	422
U	746	49	795	240	147	387	1182
V	490	33	523	150	70	220	743
W	844	54	898	240	331	571	1469
X	856	44	900	150	91	241	1141
Y	778	49	827	240	175	415	1242
Total £K	13,526	895	14,421	3000	2625	5625	20,046

Table 8.2　Company Model 3: UK Sales Target Value by Territory

Territory	New business			Renewals business			Sales target (£K)
	Product sales	Maintenance	Total	Licence renewals	Maintenance renewals	Total	
Branch Manager NW/NE	3276	222	3498	690	570	1260	4758
Branch Manager Scotland/ Ireland	898	61	959	180	108	288	1247
Regional Manager North	4174	283	4457	870	678	1548	6005
Branch Manager SE	3276	222	3498	720	738	1458	4956
Branch Manager Midlands/SW	2362	161	2523	390	395	785	3308
Regional Manager South	5638	383	6021	1110	1133	2243	8264
Regional Manager National Accounts	3714	229	3943	1020	814	1834	5777
National Sales Manager	13,526	895	14,421	3000	2625	5625	20,046

**Table 8.3   Company Model 4: UK Sales Target Value
by Branch/Region**

Products

The company's success has resulted mainly from Product A, now in its sixth year with a user base of 750. Priced at £30 thousand, Product A is its *Cash Cow*. Modifications have extended its life and it is expected to grow a further 7½% in the new year. A replacement product is in the pipeline and beta tests are scheduled for the autumn.

A less sophisticated Product B was introduced three years ago to complement Product A at remote sites but it can also operate singly at small installations. The price is £10 thousand. Product B is expected to grow at 38% in sales volume during the forthcoming year and is a *Star*, likely to maintain growth in excess of the Product A user base. Product B will be fully compatible with the proposed replacement product. A and B are supported by a training and consultancy Package C, normally sold as a contract service with an average sales value of £16 thousand. C's growth is modestly forecast at 7½% in line with A.

New and Renewal Business

Products A and B are sold as five-year licences at the end of which period a licence renewal is negotiated. In the forthcoming year this will account for 15% of the sales target in the UK. Existing users also contract to pay a maintenance charge of 10% on the licence fee each year. This represents a further 13% of the target as maintenance renewal income plus 4.5% as new maintenance. Thus new business accounts for 72% of this year's forecast turnover.

Sales Incentives

The company operates a bonus incentive scheme for all salespeople. Earnings comprise a basic salary plus incentive bonus. Territory salesmen are in a single salary grade with minimum and maximum levels. Levels are determined against overall performance and reviewed at the annual staff appraisals. Seventy percent of the basic salary is paid irrespective of performance. The remaining 30% is paid on achievement of over 90% of the cumulative sales target. The bonus scheme incorporates a points system with weighting given to the achievement of new business and overall sales performance in excess of 100% of the cumulative sales target. Thus a 90% performance earns the basic salary and 91–99% a modest bonus. Achievements of 100% and beyond earn much higher bonuses.

National account salesmen earn a higher basic salary, being one grade higher and the 'break' is at 80%. Sales targets are pitched a little higher than the budget to make provision for performance-related costs.

Salesforce

The salesforce comprises 20 territory salesmen plus five national accounts. This latter includes the creation of a new national accounts territory comprising some 16 major industrial groups in the oil, aerospace and automotive sectors. The departure of the overseas agency manager has caused a reshuffle of the sales and marketing management including the transfer of the Regional Manager North into international marketing.

Within the sales department the following staff changes have been put in train:

— Branch Manager NW/NE becomes Regional Manager North;

— Territory Salesman E becomes Branch Manager NW/NE;

— Branch Assistant NW/NE (trainee) becomes Territory Salesman E;

— Territory Salesman K becomes National Account Manager X;

— Branch Assistant L/SE (trainee) becomes Territory Salesman K.

8.4 MAJOR (NATIONAL) ACCOUNTS

8.4.1 Operating Similarities

The newly promoted national account salesman will soon appreciate that many of the tasks to be performed in managing territory X are the same as were found in running the local territory K. He/she will still be involved in operational planning, time management, territory records, prospect lists, sales forecast reports – all in the process of making sales. Thus none of the experience gained in territory K will be wasted in territory X. On the contrary, this experience is mandatory.

8.4.2 Operating Differences

The main differences encountered by the new occupant of territory X will be concerned with company size, structure, purchasing policy, geographical location and IT spending potential.

Whereas territory K comprised some 300 organisations of a size 'worth pursuing', within a radius of 75 miles from the office, territory X consists of only 16 major organisations situated all over the UK. The companies located within the boundary of territory K were mainly small or medium-sized organisations with turnovers generally between £10 million and £50 million. Territory X companies are major organisations with turnovers exceeding £250 million and some in excess of £1 billion.

8.4.3 Major Account Characteristics

Definition

Major or *national* accounts comprise the top industrial companies ranked by turnover; large government/government-related bodies; public utilities; and the principal financial institutions – banking and life assurance offices – ranked by asset value. Examples include British Aerospace, British Gas, British Coal, British Petroleum, British Rail, British Telecom, ICI, Shell, Rolls Royce, DHSS, MoD, Inland Revenue, NHS, Electricity Council, Barclays Bank and the Prudential Group. All are major employers of labour.

Size and Dispersion

By definition all national accounts are very large organisations with manufacturing, distribution, trading or service activities geographically dispersed throughout the UK. Many are multinational corporations with either British or foreign parentage and with further dispersion overseas. Most have a relatively sound growth rate through development, diversification or acquisition. Generally they are financially stable.

Organisational Variety

All major accounts will have developed organisational structures relevant to their *current* needs. Some may have retained a *centralised* organisation, where the company's growth has been in volume terms rather than through product diversification. Such companies might prefer to apply top management control through a *functional* structure. Others will be decentralised, either by geography (region) or by products. Many will use a *matrix* structure, combining both function and product forms with business units responsible for profits. Multinationals, which have multiple products and operate in multiple countries, will probably employ a matrix structure with *decentralised* profit centres whilst applying global objectives and *control of key decisions* in resource allocation and relationships with policy makers. There is no perfect design, no universal panaceas. What suits one company is alien to another. Thus an organisation's structure is *dynamic* and will change as the organisation evolves.

Commitment to Information Technology

All major accounts are heavily committed to using IT and most will have been directly involved in its evolution over many years. Thus all will have a large installed computer base with telecommunications and a correspondingly high annual IT budget of several millions of pounds.

Opposing Pressures

Major accounts organisations are subject to a variety of opposing pressures – pressures for *uniformity* (centralisation) and pressures for *decentralised* policies. As John Spackman (1988) put it:

> "The former bring economies of scale and maintain coherence, but can be inflexible and unresponsive. The latter result in agility and innovative drive, stronger motivation and commitment, but can be fragmented into competing baronies as local autonomy becomes corporate anarchy.
>
> The availability of the microcomputer to the departmental user in the large organisation has to some extent challenged the authority of the centralised data processing function. In the worst situation this has resulted in inflexible corporate DP departments operating alongside a galaxy of fragmented, unco-ordinated local systems, without technical or financial control."

Our IT salesman in territory X will need to be aware of such situations – the problems which emanate from the sheer size of major account organisations – and the strategies which help overcome them.

8.4.4 Major Account Operations

Overview

The territory management processes discussed in Chapter 7 are in general relevant to managing major accounts. If the account happened to be a large bank, the salesman would doubtless soon learn that it was departmentalised to meet the needs of specific customer groups from the commercial, institutional and retail sectors (Figure 8.4). Each might have its own major IT facility under the co-ordination of a centralised management service function. If it were an aircraft manufacturer, he/she might discern that it comprised three large operating divisions each organised as a matrix structure with the functions of engineering, purchasing, manufacturing, quality control, test and assurance linked to a series of projects (Figure 8.5). IT might well be corporate, divisional and even project based.

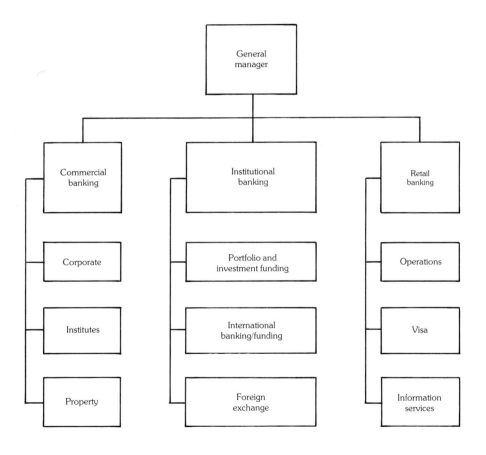

Figure 8.4   Departmental Structure

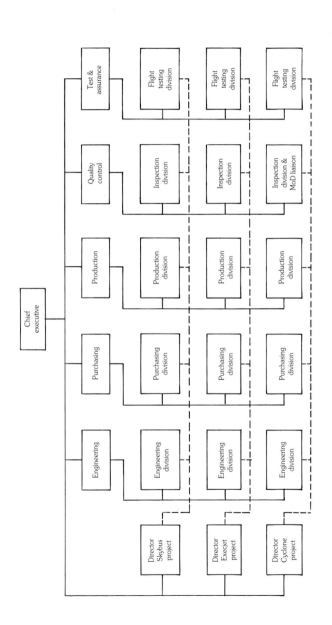

Figure 8.5 Matrix Structure

The salesman will require to develop an account development plan for each organisation.

Account Development

Key information

Firstly it is necessary to obtain information about the account in terms of finance (capital and turnover), its main business, its industry position, its organisation, board of directors, and key executives.

Sources

The ideal vehicle for key information is the annual report and accounts, together with data provided in directories such as *Kompass* or *Key British Enterprises*.

Corporate Structure

Acquaintance should be made with the head of information technology, variously styled head of management services, data processing or information systems. This person will be high in the corporate functional structure, reporting directly to the board or through the director of finance or administration. His/her department will have all the information necessary to analyse the functional areas of finance, marketing, administration and operations; the key executives; and the departmental or matrix structure of the whole organisation.

Potential Applications

Further acquaintance will provide the IT salesman with an insight into the IT strategy of the organisation – the way it responds to user needs, obtains best value for money but also maintains control over all IT support. At this stage the salesman will gain some idea of the potential for his/her product in the organisation.

Planning Guidelines

Strategic Sales Training Ltd has developed a planning guide for account development and evaluation which it teaches in its IT sales workshops. The purpose of the guidelines is to help the salesman assess the health of a major account and the account development plan in the areas of:

- management;
- application;
- planning;
- systems;
- finance.

The assessment provides an insight into the scope for business opportunities and any exposures to risk. Opportunities may have been identified as a result of detailed analysis of the account or through industry strategy. Exposures can occur through:

- not having a viable plan;
- not capitalising on business opportunities;
- competitive activity.

The guidelines comprise:

- an information questionnaire about the account, viewed as a number of business units;
- a questionnaire which seeks to evaluate *attitudes* and perceptions by the account about 'our' company.

The second questionnaire comprises statements or questions with multiple-choice answers, which the salesman must provide, each with a numeric value on a scale 0–10. Low scores represent low-risk situations. High scores are high-risk, unfavourable situations.

Armed with this indication of strengths and weaknesses our territory X salesman will then be in a position to apply sound business judgement and all the experience gained as a territory salesman in developing the account to its maximum potential. Planning guidelines are highly recommended in managing major accounts.

8.5 BRANCH SALES MANAGEMENT

8.5.1 New Skills

On promotion to the management of the NW/NE branch, the former tenant of territory E will now have the opportunity to learn (from experience) and apply many of the different skills outlined in Section 8.2.

On initial acquaintance with the job, the new branch manager may be daunted by the size of the sales target, some six times greater than territory E and the fact that achievement of the target is the collective success of six salespeople. These are the people to whom the branch manager will be *delegating* responsibility for territory sales. He/she may also be sceptical about an as yet untried ability to *discipline* former colleagues at the same level.

In practice, help is usually at hand. The prudent company will already have assessed the salesman's potential for management and arranged a suitable management training programme. Furthermore the degree of formal authority accompanying the job will be limited, especially when compared to the regional or national sales manager. For example, it is unlikely that the branch manager will have the power to recruit or dismiss staff. Nevertheless the training programme should include an appreciation of current labour law statutes, especially those relating to equal pay, sex discrimination and race relations – together with an understanding of codes of practice on grievance and dispute procedures and of the employment of disabled persons. The job of branch manager will be the ideal proving ground for more senior appointments later.

8.5.2 Managing a Branch

Responsibilities

The key tasks assigned to the branch manager will comprise:

- involvement in the selection of new staff;

- induction, training and appraisal of sales trainees;

- motivation and control of territory salespeople;

- monitoring of performance of all salespeople with identification of strengths, weaknesses and recommendations for improvement;

- approval of major sales proposals;

- allocation of sales targets to individual territories;

- co-ordination of requests for technical and other support;

- provision and management of branch administration services;

- authorisation of all branch expenditure within the budget;

- regular reporting of prospects, sales forecasts and achievements.

These tasks are essential to the branch manager's prime responsibility:

– securing the branch sales target by period, quarter and year end.

Activities

In undertaking the key tasks, the branch manager will allocate his/her time among the following activities:

Coaching

The first five tasks in 'Responsibilities' (above) are concerned with coaching and this is the most important activity. It involves making sales visits with salesmen, appraising their performance in 'kerbside counsell-ing', arranging appropriate training and generally acquainting each individual with the role of the branch, their place in it, and their responsibilities – which will be monitored. The test of the manager's leadership will be the response from the salesmen, which will depend *inter alia* on the achievability of the target and their regard for the manager's abilities. Within this activity is also a regular dialogue with the sales training manager on individual training needs.

Planning

Like the territory salesmen, the branch manager will submit an operational plan for the year ahead, bringing together all the individual territory plans. However this plan will also include a phased budget of branch costs, against which the branch manager will be measured.

Branch Progress Meetings

In convening period end progress meetings, the branch manager will have the opportunity to 'take stock', provide training, introduce new products or enhancements, and above all obtain feedback from the field. The attitudes of those attending will be a further indication of the manager's rating with the sales staff. Thus it is essential that the sessions be interactive, with all staff given the opportunity to make a contribution.

Budgeting

This annual process, done in tandem with the operational plan, will include sales targets and expenditure budgets. Both will be flexed monthly and quarterly. Expenditure budgets will include all travel, subsistence, training and external costs associated with the sales staff together with all establishment expenses of the branch. In this latter respect only controllable costs will be involved such as telephones, temporary staff and consumables. Fixed or other costs outside the responsibility of the branch manager will be included in corporate budgets and controlled by the *functional* manager, the accountant.

Branch Administration

This activity can be most time consuming. Not only will it include all secretarial services, stock control and general office management but possibly a local maintenance service with workshops, garage and parts stock facilities. If the branch is large, the services of an office manager will be necessary to release the branch manager for more sales-oriented tasks.

Regional Progress Meetings

The branch manager will be expected to make a contribution to higher level progress meetings, at which time he/she will table the branch progress report, provide feedback on outstanding sales, unusual sales, lost sales and problems reported from the field. Information gleaned at these meetings on products, pricing and other policies will be relayed to the salesforce at the next branch meeting.

An understanding of leadership, control, communication, discipline, delegation and all the other management skills will soon be developed through practical experience in the above activities.

8.6 REGIONAL SALES MANAGEMENT

8.6.1 Higher Responsibility and Authority

The regional sales manager is a very senior member of the marketing and sales hierarchy, responsible for making a major contribution to the company revenue. The former branch manager will soon be aware that the job goes far beyond that of leading salespeople to achieve sales objectives.

In the company model, the Regional Manager North carries almost one-third of the UK sales target. But the job also includes responsibility for the provision and allocation of all the resources necessary to sustain the branches. These resources, which include people, premises, equipment and services, cost a deal of money. Thus the regional manager will be closely involved in the *budgetary control* and management accounting process.

These and other activities will require a degree of *negotiating* skills, not only with subordinate staff but in dealings with the marketing group and elsewhere in the organisation. As defender of the region, he/she may be competing with other parts of the group for marketing services. The work will also include dialogues with the line managers outside marketing, who are responsible for the financial, legal, personnel, product development and other functions of the organisation.

In a matrix-driven organisation the regional manager will be in regular contact with the business managers responsible for the profitability of product-based business units. Business managers will wish to see a high return from their investment in sales costs which they are paying, albeit through internal transfers, to the marketing and sales group.

Thus the regional manager has a dual commitment. Responsibility to the sales manager for achieving the sales target as a corporate goal, and also to the business managers (the internal customers) for providing value for money. Clearly the role of the manager has now moved away from that of coach to that of senior executive. However the regional manager should not distance him/herself from the salesmen, nor create an ivory tower image. It is important to visit the branches, attend some of their progress meetings, be seen to have an 'open door' and above all to be a senior manager who is 'on their side'.

The added responsibilities will carry with them a correspondingly higher level of designated *authority*. Within legal and corporate rules this will include the power to engage and dismiss staff and to make major decisions involving the commitment of resources, special prices and so on.

8.6.2 Managing a Region

Responsibilities

The prime responsibility of a regional manager is to achieve the regional sales target and to maintain a high level of customer satisfaction within an agreed cost budget. This implies the provision of:

— an effective and motivated salesforce;

— products which are relevant and available;

— technical support;

— an efficient branch operation.

Key Tasks

In discharging these responsibilities the regional manager will be assigned the following key tasks:

— motivation of all branch managers in the region;

— selection of all sales staff, including trainees;

— appointment of branch managers;

— approval of all other appointments in the branches;

— allocation of branch sales targets by product units and value;

— resolution of all branch staff conflicts;

— relaying of field intelligence (feedback);

— approval of branch managers' expenses;

— contribution to marketing group policy and progress meetings;

— appraisal of all staff annually.

Activities

Thus the regional manager will divide his/her time between:

Branch Visits

A continuous dialogue with each branch manager will do much to demonstrate higher level support and an ability to resolve issues which are inhibiting branch sales or good customer relations. These might include a willingness to visit a dissatisfied user; to arbitrate in a territory sales dispute; secure special technical support; or arrange temporary staff transfers in the event of prolonged sickness. Attendance at, say, four branch progress meetings each year will do much to boost the branch manager and to motivate the branch salesmen.

Personnel Liaison

Co-operation with the personnel manager will be required in situations such as:

- sales staff selection (see Section 5.2);

- other staff appointments;

- annual staff appraisal process;

- disciplinary action;

- grievance;

- dismissal.

Planning and Budgeting

Operational planning will extend beyond that of collating the branch plans into a composite regional plan. Other inputs will include phased product and product enhancement releases which are to be reflected in flexed sales targets. Further differences will include market segmentation strategies that have been agreed by the marketing group and business managers. Planned growth will also be reflected in the budget, an integral part of the regional operations plan. This will be agreed with the accountant and approved by the sales manager.

Regional Progress Meetings

These will be convened each period, shortly after branch progress meetings to allow branch managers time to prepare their reports. The occasional attendance of the sales manager should be encouraged. The agenda should include a review of:

- branch managers' progress reports on activity levels, cumulative performance against target, territory feedback, problems and highlights;

- regional manager's report on group policy, new products, enhancements, prices, conditions of sale, etc;

- promotional events;

- arrangements for sales conferences and training;

- support;

- publicity;

- training needs.

Support Liaison

At a tactical level the regional manager will meet regularly with the technical support manager to ensure that all pre- and post-sales requirements are met.

Similar dialogues will occur with the marketing services manager on matters such as the timely provision of sales literature, price list changes and promotional events such as national exhibitions or mail-shots.

Group Management Meetings

The regional manager will meet regularly with the sales manager, formally or informally according to the latter's style. During such sessions the sales manager will be acquainted with all regional progress, problems and branch feedback. In his turn the sales manager will apprise the regional manager of any policy changes and his assessment of regional perform-ance.

However the regional manager is likely to be expected to make a positive contribution to marketing group meetings, convened by the marketing director quarterly. At these meetings, attended by *all* marketing group managers, higher level topics will be addressed, including:

— economic and other market influences;

— future direction;

— finance;

— resources;

— organisation and staffing;

— job skills;

— incentives.

8.7 NATIONAL SALES MANAGEMENT

8.7.1 Principal Role

The main responsibilities of the national sales manager are to:

— plan and organise the company's sales;

— motivate the salesforce;

- develop job skills;

- contribute to the marketing activity;

- maintain the corporate image.

8.7.2 Modus Operandi

In our company model the sales manager has three regional managers and a sales training manager reporting to him. In practice this could be much larger. Some IT companies have over 400 salespeople, many more branches and perhaps 10 regions. Although applying all the management activities referred to in Section 8.2.2, the sales manager will be particularly concerned with the following three:

- *delegation* to the regional managers;

- *negotiation* with the marketing group, business managers and functional peers;

- *motivation* of the department.

Planning and Organisation

Planning at this level is a flexible process which responds to external influences, internal policy and market feedback. External influences (Section 3.1) are those outside the company's control.

The sales operation plan will also relate to the *corporate plan*, which will have been promulgated to the sales manager by the marketing director, finance director and business managers. Familiar with the parameters for the year ahead, the sales manager will issue planning guidelines to the regional managers covering the essential topics of unit sales requirements, manpower, resource needs and costs. Several iterations will doubtless be required before the operational plans are agreed and assembled into the sales plan. The sales plan will also reflect any organisational changes needed in the ensuing year. For example, the introduction of a major new product for the insurance sector might require the setting up of a new national account territory.

Motivation

Motivating the salesforce is probably the most difficult task of the sales manager. Not only do people react differently to the same stimuli but the motivation process is quite complex. It is concerned with those factors that stimulate human behaviour, how behaviour is directed, and how it can be maintained. Some of the salesmen may be motivated by money and what it will buy, others by achieving ever higher figures year after year, and some by the 'thrill of the chase'. Thus the sales manager will need to address motivation in some depth by studying speculations such as Maslow's Need Hierarchy; Need/Achievement Theory; Hertzburg's Motivation/Hygiene Theory; Expectancy/Valence Theory; and more recent research into the 'motivation–performance–satisfaction' relationship.

Most companies will employ some form of bonus incentive scheme with financial rewards based on continuous achievement of the sales target. Others might introduce the '100% club', membership of which is exclusive to those who achieved their sales target in the previous year. Club membership might carry benefits such as an invitation to attend its annual convention abroad; club status based purely on the percentage performance achieved; and special club insignia.

Developing Job Skills

In conjunction with the regional managers, the sales manager will review the training requirements–general and individual–of the whole salesforce, including branch secretarial staff. This will be discussed with the sales training manager so that a programme can be arranged for the year ahead, covering all the topics discussed in Section 6.2 and further subjects such as using the telephone effectively. The latter would be valuable to all staff likely to speak to customers.

As part of the annual appraisal, the sales manager should also be in a position to identify future candidates for promotion. Consideration might then be given to seconding such people into other parts of the organisation as part of a development process – a grooming for future management.

Contribution to the Marketing Activity

The most important input to marketing that the sales manager can bring is the mood of the customers. Feedback released through the branches and regions will provide marketing with priceless information on needs, preferences, the impact of competition and change. Group management meetings are the ideal vehicles for raising such issues.

Maintain the Corporate Image

Although the corporate image is, in the main, reflected through the marketing processes – in particular through logos, company and product themes on all company material – the sales manager has a part to play.

When a new product is released, or a company acquisition concluded, the sales manager may well be involved in the press conference or at a series of regional presentations. Thus the sales manager *must* be a good presenter, not only to provide the right image in public but to demonstrate by example the image that every member of the salesforce would wish to emulate. Above all the sales manager is required to set behavioural standards for the salesforce and, through delegation and example, ensure that these standards are maintained.

8.8 DIRECTOR OF MARKETING

8.8.1 Perspective

The head of the marketing function is a very senior manager in any company and as such is required to demonstrate an array of business skills – skills which will be directed towards business strategy, through group management and high-level decision making. Candidates for this post will have developed many such skills in different, usually lower management echelons. Likely sources will include marketing services, sales, overseas sales and technical support managers.

In a matrix-driven organisation any of the product business managers might apply. Those with a business or management degree will have an edge since their skills will have been developed in a *systematic* way. For example the Business Skills Programme at Manchester Polytechnic (Appendix 5) *progresses* the student through:

1 self-knowledge skills;

2 interpersonal skills;

3 group working skills;

4 business social skills;

5 managerial skills;

6 communication skills;

7 research skills;

8 project skills;

9   commercial skills;

10 political and PR skills.

All are relevant to the job of managing the marketing function.

The aim of this book is *not* to attempt to teach the practice of management. There are far more appropriate avenues for learning the discipline through the business faculties and the commercial book world. Rather the objective here is to provide the reader with a *flavour* of this exacting job and to highlight some of the tasks within its remit.

8.8.2 Business Strategy

Strategy is when you are out of ammunition, but keep right on firing so that the enemy won't know.

– author unknown

The three levels of management outlined thus far (Sections 8.5–8.7) are in the main concerned with *tactics*. Their role is to guide the salesforce towards achieving the corporate objectives and to use available resources effectively.

As a member of the top executive, much of the marketing director's attention will be focussed on business strategy, otherwise described as the *concept of the firm's business*. This strategic activity helps determine the course the company should take towards achieving its economic and social objectives.

Leading authorities in management practice tell us that the concept of the firm's business requires a 'common denominator' – a relationship between current and future products and their markets. This enables the outside world to perceive what the firm is about and where it is going. They further propose that this common thread can be specified through an understanding of four of the firm's characteristics – its product/market scope, its growth vector, its competitive advantage, and its synergy (Ansoff, 1968).

Product/Market Scope

Here the marketing director will be defining those market segments to which the company's products are presently confined. A variety of statistics and market forecast data is usually available.

Growth Vector

The marketing director will also be measuring the direction in which the company is moving with its current product/market policy. To aid in this assessment of growth potential, he/she will be concerned with factors such as market penetration, new products and the scope for acquisitions and diversification.

Competitive Advantage

In this the marketing director will be identifying those features of the company's products and services which give the firm a strong competitive edge.

Synergy

Finally he/she will be involved in the process of measuring the firm's ability to launch new products successfully.

In assessing the individual skills and resources which make up the firm's *competence*, the marketing director will be particularly concerned with marketing issues such as the ability to create product acceptance, effective promotion, accurate sales forecasting, sales and distribution resources, contract administration and adequate customer support.

8.8.3 Decision Making

> *The buck stops here.*
>
> – sign on the desk of Harry S Truman

In expressing the firm's business strategy, the marketing director will, like his subordinate managers, be undertaking a range of communicative activities requiring leadership, motivation and control. These powers of communication will be tested not just within marketing but in the executive forum.

The keystone of all management activities at this level is *decision making*. It comes in three forms:

Strategic Decisions

Strongly influenced by external factors such as the economic climate and strength of the competition, they include such things as:

- deciding the product mix;
- deciding the market to which it will sell;
- deciding whether the company has the capability to venture into new markets.

Thus all the activities discussed in Section 8.8.2 will require the marketing director to take strategic decisions in order to produce the best possible resource allocation pattern.

Operating Decisions

For the marketing director these will include:

- deciding the pricing policy;
- deciding the marketing policy;
- deciding on relevant expenditure levels.

Administrative Decisions

These are concerned mainly with the *organisation* of the firm's marketing resources, in particular the *structuring* of authority and information flows, deciding on distribution channels, and deciding where to locate facilities. Administrative decisions are also required for the acquisition and development of resources.

8.8.4 Group Management

Much of the analysis required for strategic decision making will be provided from within the marketing group. Thus armed with the right information the marketing director is in a position to contribute to the firm's business strategy with the co-operation of his or her executive peers in finance, operations and other functional groups.

However the provision of accurate and timely information is but one reflection of an efficient marketing and sales group for which he/she is also ultimately responsible. Therefore at the operational and administration levels, the marketing director will delegate, motivate, monitor and control all his/her subordinate, albeit senior, managers in the group, including the national sales manager, technical support manager and marketing services manager (Figure 3.1).

In some IT companies a significant proportion of revenues is earned overseas and this adds a further dimension to the marketing director's remit. At a tactical level this includes responsibility for the performance of overseas distributors and agents normally delegated to agency managers.

8.8.5 Conclusion

Taking responsibility for all the activities discussed in Chapter 3 – and deciding what business the firm is in – is clearly a complex and often daunting prospect. Few salesmen will reach, or wish to reach, this level of management. Those seeking it as their ultimate career goal will need to develop a host of business skills, secure a track record, work extremely hard, and look for opportunities. Those who do not make it will still find *selling* IT a vastly rewarding job, whether at territory, national account, branch, regional or sales manager level.

I wish them every success!

Part 4
Support

Give us the tools and we will finish the job.
— Winston Churchill (1941)

9 Support

9.1 DUAL NEED

In Chapter 4 it was emphasised that the prime role of the IT salesman is to earn and protect the company's revenues. To achieve this goal he/she will require a fair degree of company support before a sale is concluded, during the implementation period, and long after the product has been working on site. In the complex IT solution business, such support is essential if the salesman is to make new business and retain (and develop) existing accounts.

Successful retention of the customer base is almost directly proportional to the level and quality of customer service. Thus all post-sales support is a need not only of the client but also of the salesman. Indeed all successful IT suppliers invest heavily in customer support services. Here are but four examples:

- IBM has five corporate goals, not least of which is 'to enhance our customer partnerships'. Peters and Waterman (1982) state that IBM's dominance rests on its commitment to service. This policy extends to the secondment of some of its best salesmen as assistants to the company's top officers. During such typical three-year stints they have one job – answering every customer complaint within 24 hours!

- Honeywell-Bull is similarly dedicated to its 'Total Service' capability, accepting the premise that no computer system is infallible – that there always remains the chance that hardware problems and software faults will occur. Honeywell is committed to providing high-quality cover for all eventualities.

— Here in the UK, Unisys maintains a vast residential customer education centre with, *inter alia*, 34 classrooms supported by 18 computer laboratories and computer equipment worth some £2 million.

— NCR extends its customer support way beyond that of hardware and software maintenance. Its service includes consultants who can guide a new customer through a project on time and to a high-quality level and provide expertise as required in implementing leading edge solutions.

9.2 CUSTOMER SERVICES

9.2.1 Maintenance

A range of maintenance contracts covering all computer hardware is offered to the IT user. The speed of response to a hardware fault will depend partly on the level of maintenance accepted by the customer. Many users prefer the security of a short-time response, typically within four hours, whilst others might opt for a basic, fault-finding, time and materials agreement.

   Maintenance infers access to the system and the provision of a site engineer. Thus most suppliers locate their field engineers at strategic regional offices.

9.2.2 Support

Hot Line

Responsible IT suppliers maintain a hot-line response centre into which all reported faults, hardware and software, are logged. The function of the centre is to find out firstly whether the fault is in the hardware or software and secondly whether or not the problem is unique. If the problem has been addressed and solved previously, then a 'fix' will doubtless be implemented immediately. If unique then a diagnostic process is under-taken, using all the technical data available to the centre, sometimes requiring access to overseas facilities. A temporary 'fix' will be attempted to, at least, circumvent the fault. If a software fault now corrected is likely to recur at other sites then a software release notice will be issued so that all users may avoid the problem.

Product Changes

Improvements, particularly to standard software, occur continuously. Thus periodically these are consolidated into a new version of the product and despatched to users. Software support includes the provision of replacement pages to the user manuals with adequate description of the new features and facilities.

Remote Links

On occasions the IT supplier will wish to access the customer's computer system remotely. Such interrogation can help diagnose and remove faults, especially software faults. Access should always be under the control of the user.

Consultancy

Some IT suppliers offer the services of their consultants to help a client manage a project. These people will be experienced both in the company's products and in implementing leading edge solutions in similar industries. They can also be of help in determining the choice of other proprietary software, which could be used to advantage, and also acting as stand-ins for key user personnel. Sometimes consultants conduct site audits to remove malpractices affecting the system's performance or security.

Implementation

Some major suppliers of systems will make available to the new user a range of implementation services in the areas of:

- planning of training needs, site arrangements, security and systems administration and end-user familiarisation;
- technical assistance in the creation of master files and databases; running parallel systems; writing procedure instructions and reviewing progress.

Education and Training

Although the customer can (and usually will) employ outside specialists for both professional training and end-user education, much will rest with the supplier. In particular technical courses covering systems software and operating regimes will be provided for the users' IT management, administrators, systems designers, database specialists, programmers and operating staff. Some IT suppliers will go much further, extending their training curricula to all aspects of IT and provide courses for line managers and other end-users.

Contingency Planning

IT suppliers will always wish to help a client in extreme emergency situations involving system collapse. Contingency planning support includes provision of direct non-mains switchboard telephone lines; security copies of files at remote sites; standard telecommunications and network interfaces; fall-back procedures; systems re-start procedures; and stand-by generators.

User Group Liaison

Customers of a particular supplier frequently form their own independent users' association, with an elected council. Such groups meet regularly, exchange information and convey a collective viewpoint to the supplier. Most suppliers welcome such groups and provide a small liaison team to co-operate to mutual advantage.

Consultant Liaison

Since many users/prospective users employ specialist consultants it pays IT suppliers to maintain a consultant liaison team to provide regular information on product releases and services.

9.3 SALES SUPPORT

To function effectively the IT salesman will require *direct* support in five areas:

- technical;

- marketing;

- management;

- administration;

- training.

9.3.1 Technical Support

Beyond the anticipated customer support outlined in Section 9.2, direct technical back-up will be required during the various stages of the sales cycle. This could occur for example when the *recommender* (IT manager) brings to a meeting his chief programmer (*influencer*) to hammer out in depth a technical feature of the proposed system. This could require a level of product and computing knowledge beyond the skills of the salesman.

In software selling, the services of a technical support consultant are invaluable in mounting a *trial* of a product at the customer's site. The successful conclusion of the trial normally heralds the placement of an order, but this will only occur through the user having been given a full understanding of the product's application and capability.

Finally, technical support is frequently sought to handle serious objections. If the salesman cannot answer the objection at the time, but has the *means* to provide the answer, then the client will be impressed.

9.3.2 Marketing Support

All the activities within the marketing mix, described in Chapter 3, will be of *indirect* value to the salesman. However the following *direct* marketing aids are essential:

Promotion

These will include provision of:

- beta test sites for the acceptance proving of new products in the territory;
- new product information to users and selected prospects;
- a mailing list service for local sales campaigns;
- exhibition stands and material for national and local events together with the routeing of all enquiries to relevant salesmen;
- similar circulation of responses to national mail-shots;
- telemarketing services for the 'part qualification' of prospective customers by different product lines;
- standard demonstration scripts for product presentations.

Publicity

This includes an adequate supply of sales material for inclusion in the portfolio, such as:

- product sales literature;
- company annual report and summary of achievements;
- copies of all advertising material;
- notice of significant or unusual sales;
- copies of major press releases;
- technical manuals for all products;
- company insignia.

Other

Other necessary material includes:

- product marketing information sheets, giving the latest data or current products/features and price changes; advance notice of new product releases and programmes of future promotional events;
- price lists with all possible permutations;
- information on competitive activity and products.

9.3.3 Management Support

As implied in Chapter 8, some reliance will be placed on the counselling and direct support of the branch or regional manager on sales visits and in the pursuit of resources. Further indirect support should be forthcoming at branch sales meetings when ideas and experiences are exchanged.

9.3.4 Sales Administration

The salesman will depend on sales administration for the processing of all orders, the raising of invoices and the correct allocation of such sales to the territory. Often the same department will manage any incentive scheme involving commission or bonus payments. These will be based on its period sales tabulations by territory, which will show the cumulative performance, and target, which will enable the salesman to confirm (or challenge) the incentive payment due.

9.3.5 Training Support

Finally the provision of the services of a sales training manager will help identify individual sales, product, technical and business training needs. These will be organised in the annual training programme. At a general level, sales and product training should feature in national sales conferences.

Appendix 1

Glossary

Application A job or task which can be performed using a computer system.

Application program A set of computer instructions which are executed by the computer to perform some task directly associated with an application.

Application program generator (APG) A class of software products offered as an addition or alternative to other software products concerned with producing data processing applications. The main objective of the APG is to enable such applications to be produced more easily, cheaply and quickly.

Architecture A framework for a computer or communications system which defines its function, interfaces and procedures.

Assembler A program that takes as input a program written in assembly language and translates it into machine code or relocatable code.

Bandwidth The lower and upper frequencies which are available for transmission.

Broadband A method of using a transmission medium having a wide frequency bandwidth. In it several signals can be carried simultaneously by allocating different channels to separate the frequency bands.

Channel

A means of transporting information signals. Several channels can share the same physical circuit.

Chip

A piece of silicon, usually about a quarter of an inch square, carrying all the components which will make up all or part of a micro-computer.

Comité Consultatif International Télégraphique et Téléphonique (CCITT)

The international body through which the national telecommunications bodies co-ordinate their activities.

Communication

The process of transmitting meanings from sender to receiver.

Compiler

A program that translates high-level language into absolute code or sometimes into assembly language. The input to the compiler (the source code) is a description of an algorithm or program in a problem-oriented language; its output (the object code) is an equivalent description of the algorithm in a machine-oriented language.

Computer Aided Design (CAD)

The use of computers in solving mechanical engineering design problems; for example, plotting the shape of a car or determining the contours of car bodies.

Computer Aided Manufacture (CAM)

The use of computers to help make manufacturing decisions and/or to control manufacturing (production line) operations.

Computerised Numerical Control (CNC)

The computerised control of a manufacturing operation (welding, cutting, machining, lifting) in an essentially automatic mode by means of coded instructions in numeric form.

Concentration   The function of channelling information from a number of users on to a small number of higher capacity lines. A *concentrator* is the device which performs the function and it is generally reprogrammable (compare with *multiplexing*).

Convergence   The merging of office, computing and communications technologies.

Database   An organised collection of information in which data is available to all systems, instead of each application having its own individual collection.

Decentralisation   A system of management in which a great deal of decision making authority is delegated to lower levels of the hierarchy.

Digital data network   See *public data network*.

Distributed database   One organised collection of data which has been subdivided or copied, and distributed amongst several different locations in a distributed system.

Distributed system   An information processing system in which a number of individual processors at different locations are linked together so that they can co-operate.

Electronic mail   The distribution of mail by electronic means.

End-user   A person who uses an information processing system.

Esteem needs   The need to feel important and to receive recognition.

Expectancy   A term used in expectancy−valence theory,
                                  referring to the perceived probability of attain-
                                  ing a first-level outcome.

Extrinsic rewards   External rewards such as money, conditions
                                  of employment and job security.

Fibre optics   A process of transmitting data by modulating
                                  a light source and transmitting light (rather
                                  than electric signal) along a glass fibre cable.
                                  Very high bandwidths are achieved and optic
                                  fibres are immune to electrical interference
                                  and less susceptible to unauthorised eaves-
                                  droppers.

File   An organised collection of data records which
                                  can be accessed by name.

Functional organisation   The organisation of an enterprise around the
                                  basic activities (functions) which the enter-
                                  prise must perform, such as production,
                                  marketing, finance and administration.

Gateway   A computer system or exchange in one
                                  network which allows access to and from
                                  another network.

High-level Data Link   A protocol designed for data transmission
Control (HDLC)   which does not use control characters and is
                                  data independent.

Host   A computer system on which applications can
                                  be executed and which also provides a service
                                  to users of a computer network.

Information processor   A computer system which provides comput-
                                  ing, data storage and data manipulation
                                  services for end-user applications.

Information System (IS)   A system concerned with all the operations and procedures for handling information.

Interface   A boundary between two devices or two
                                     pieces of software across which the form and
                                     functions of the signals which pass it are
                                     specified.

Interfacing devices   Devices linking the user directly with the
                                     computer.

International   The body which exists to promote the de-
Organization for   velopment of standards throughout the
Standardization (ISO)   world. Membership consists of national orga-
                                     nisations which are most representative of
                                     standardisation in their countries.

Intrinsic rewards   Internal rewards such as challenge, feelings of
                                     accomplishment and recognition for a job well
                                     done.

Layer   A set of logically related functions which are
                                     grouped together. Interfaces to and from the
                                     layer can be standardised but not the ways
                                     the internal functions are performed.

Local Area Network   A data transmission system intended to link
(LAN)   computers and associated devices within a
                                     restricted geographical area. The two princip-
                                     al research systems which have influenced
                                     LAN development are the Cambridge Ring
                                     (University of Cambridge) and Ethernet
                                     (Xerox Corporation).

Manufacturing   A specification which defines the use of
Automation Protocol   international standards within the manufac-
(MAP)   turing industry to solve the problems of
                                     getting incompatible equipment to communi-
                                     cate.

Matrix organisation   A hybrid combination of both product and

functional structures. Product managers rel
on the functional managers for support and
assistance, since the former have no line
authority.

Message

A logically related collection of data to be
moved.

Modem

A device which converts digital systems into
analogue or varying electrical signals for
transmission over normal telephone lines.
The modem also performs the reverse
function.

Multiplexing

The use of a single physical link for two or
more simultaneous separate transmissions. A
multiplexer is the device which performs this
function. It is not usually programmable by
the user.

Multitasking

The operation of simultaneously executing a
main task or sub-tasks that are either inter-
leaved (by a single processor) or executed
concurrently (by a multiplexer).

Node

A point at which two or more communications lines meet. Usually applied to a computer or switching device situated at this position.

On-line system

A computing system which permits data to be
entered directly into the system through a
terminal, and output to be made available
directly where it is needed.

**Open Systems Inter-
connection (OSI)**

Standardised procedures for the exchange of
information between terminals, computers,
people, networks, *etc*, which are accessible to
one another by virtue of their mutual use of
these procedures.

Organisational behaviour

An academic discipline concerned with describing, understanding, predicting and controlling human behaviour in an organisational environment.

PABX

Private Automatic Branch Exchange: a sophisticated, processor-controlled private telephone exchange.

Packet

A block of data with a defined format containing control and data fields.

Packet switching

A term used in a data transmission network which is designed to carry the data in the form of packets. The data in packets is passed to the network, and devices within it use the control information to transmit the packet to the correct destination.

Personality

An individual's characteristics and behaviours, organised in such a way as to reflect the unique adjustment the person makes to his or her environment.

Plug compatible

A term used to describe peripheral devices, which are compatible (will plug in) with the specified products of mainstream computer manufacturers.

Polling

A process whereby terminals are invited one at a time to transmit information.

Post, Telegraph and Telephone administration (PTT)

A general term to denote a supplier of telecommunication services.

Product departmentalisation

The organisation of an enterprise around its major product lines.

Protocol

A set of rules to ensure a meaningful

communication between co-operating partners.

Public data network   A communication system which is intended for transmission of digital data, and which is available to anyone wishing to subscribe to it.

Real-time   An expression used to refer to any system in which the processing of data input to obtain a result occurs virtually simultaneously with the event generating the data. Effectively describes process control and airline booking systems.

Resource-conversion process   The process of maximising the profitability of current operations.

Rewards   See *Extrinsic* and *Intrinsic rewards.*

Robot   A programmable device capable of performing physical operations involving three-dimensional movement.

Robotics   The design or construction of robots.

Safety needs   Needs for security and stability, often satisfied by the provision of health plans, pension packages, life cover and other fringe benefits.

Satellite processor   A computer system which has a subsidiary role in a distributed system.

Self-actualisation needs   The desire to become more and more what one is; to become everything one is capable of becoming.

Skill   The level of proficiency one has in performing a specific task.

Software engineering   The application of an appropriate set of techniques and tools for the whole process of software production, which enables a project team to set and meet its goals within an acceptable cost and timescale.

Status

The relative ranking of an individual in an organisation or group.

Switching

In computer or communications networks, switching is the process by which services or data are directed to the appropriate user.

System

A collection of computers, associated software, peripherals, terminals, human users, etc, which form an autonomous whole, capable of information processing.

Terminal

A device which allows an end-user to input data and receive it from a computer system.

Transaction processing

The entering of records of events into information processing systems as each event occurs.

Valence

A term used in expectancy–valence theory. It refers to a person's preference for a particular outcome.

Values

Beliefs people have which shape their views of what is important, good or bad, right or wrong.

von Neumann (Architecture)

A computer design approach containing:

- a single computing element that incorporates a processor, communication and memory;
- a linear organisation of fixed-size memory cells;
- a one-level address space of memory cells;

- a one-level machine language (instructions performing simple operations on simple operands);

- a sequential centralised control of computation;

- a primitive input/output capability.

V-Series

The CCITT recommendations for data transmission over telephone (ie analogue) networks.

Word processing

A combination of text handling and computing.

Workstation

A terminal at which certain types of (business-related) work is performed.

X-Series

The CCITT recommendations for data transmission over digital data networks.

Appendix 2

Bibliography

Ansoff H I, Concept of the firm's business and the common thread, *Corporate Strategy*, Penguin, 1968, pp 94–101

Ansoff H I, Structure of business decisions, *Corporate Strategy*, Penguin, 1968, pp 17–19

Ashworth J M, *Opening Address*, (NCC Members' Conference), Gleneagles, 31 October 1985

Business Monitor PA1003, *Size Analysis of UK Businesses*, Business Statistics Office, HMSO, 1986

Civil Service Year Book, HMSO, 1985

Computing Services Association, *Annual Report 1987*

Crowe D, Your just desserts: assessing them and getting them, *The Times*, 25 August 1987

D'Agapeyeff A, *Expert Systems, Fifth Generation and UK Suppliers*, NCC Publications, 1983

Davis A, *Selling Professional Services*, NCC Publications, 1984

Hedley B, Strategy and the business portfolio, *Long Range Planning*, February 1977, p 12

Hodgetts R M, Altman S, Integrative motivation model, *Organisational Behaviour*, W B Saunders, 1979

International Organization for Standardization (ISO 2382 Part 1), *Definition of Operating System*, ISO, 1984

Manchester Polytechnic Faculty of Management and Business, *Group Needs*, 1987

Maslow A H, *Motivation and Personality*, Harper and Row, 1954

NCC, *Computer Services Index*, 1988

NCC, *Computer Systems Overview*, 1984

NCC, *Computing Decisions*, 1987

NCC, *Implications of Information Technology*, NCC Training Course Package

NCC, *Information Technology Trends*, 1987

NCC, *Introduction to Data Processing Syllabus*, NCC Training, 1988

NCC, *Salaries and Staff Issues in Computing*, 1987

OPQ Concept 3 Profile Chart, *Personality Testing*, Saville and Holdsworth, 1984

Pedder Associates, Census of UK computer systems, *Computing*, 16 November 1987, p 20

Peters T S, Waterman Jr R H, *In Search of Excellence*, Harper and Row, 1982, p 159

Simons G L, *Towards Fifth-Generation Computers*, NCC Publications, 1983

Spackman J, How to avoid the worst, Extract from paper delivered at *Computer Weekly*'s IT perspectives conference, *Computer Weekly*, 21 January 1988, pp 18–19

Strategic Sales Training, *Account Development Planning Guide*

Strategic Sales Training, *Presenting a Proposal for Change*

Strategic Sales Training, *Prospect Ranking Techniques*

Strategic Sales Training, *Qualification Criteria*

Strategic Sales Training, *Sales Training Workshop Syllabus*

Strategic Sales Training, *Satisfying Needs and Concerns*

Telecommunications Industry Research Centre, FT survey of world telecommunications, *Financial Times*, 19 October 1987, p 24

The Times 80 earnings table, *The Times*, 24 August 1987, p 8

Appendix 3

K Shoes: a Case Study

K Shoes could be considered to be fairly typical of a medium-sized, long-established company with a lengthy history of IT activity. Having said that, there is no such thing as a typical company, any more than there is an average man or woman. The peculiarities of the marketplace, the characteristics of the product and the idiosyncracies of management all lead to a degree of local uniqueness, which is reflected in the business systems.

BUSINESS ENVIRONMENT

K Shoes is in the business of manufacturing, distributing and retailing high-quality branded footwear, mainly in the domestic market. Total 1987 turnover was c £100 million *pa*, with a good trading profit and return on capital employed.

Since the early 1950s, the company has expanded from a family-owned concern (founded in 1842) to a major player in the branded footwear scene. Periods in which expansion was most rapid were in 1965–1975, and again since joining the C & J Clark Group in 1982. The company has retained operational autonomy within the C & J Clark Group.

The marketplace is limited in terms of total consumption and is under pressure from imports. Success is dependent on increasing market share; this can only be achieved by offering better products, better quality and better service in a competitive market.

The product ranges on offer reflect the fashionable nature of the marketplace, with a high rate of change and widely varying sales demand cycles. These are necessary to meet the two seasons per year needs of retailers. The need to offer numerous colour, width and size combinations results in a large number of discrete items (c 30,000 per season); these items are sold through 260 wholly owned shops and approximately 3000 other outlets. Total sales are just over five million pairs *pa*.

Manufacturing capacity is in nine factory units spread across southern Cumbria. There is a limited amount of interchangeability between units. The main business requirement is to provide production schedules which make effective use of the available capacity under the impact of widely varying seasonal sales demands.

IT HISTORY

The history of IT developments reflects the imperatives of the business environment and the growth of the company. It can best be described in four areas of systems development.

1938–1967: Unit Record Systems

From the earliest days punched cards were used to represent available stock, for order processing, and for invoice preparation. By 1967 these systems were too cumbersome to cope with the expanding business.

1967–1972: 1st Generation Mainframe Systems

Fairly simple batch, serial file systems were developed based on previous experiences with unit record systems. These coped well with the initial expansion of the business and were themselves expanded to include production planning, material planning and retail functions. However by 1970 it was clear that neither the equipment nor the technology in use would support the changing needs of the company over a 5–8-year horizon.

1971–1985: 2nd Generation Mainframe Systems (ICL)

The key to systems developments in this period was the use of disk-based, integrated data files accessed through data handling software. This software, developed in house, provided data transparency and multiple access to files, mapped through a data dictionary.

Most of the principal functions covered in the previous stage were re-written in this new environment by the end of 1973 and subsequently many new systems were introduced to cover the remaining key business functions. These systems were still essentially batch processing, but with many more simultaneous processes; a limited amount of on-line access was provided.

This environment has stood the test of time, having coped successfully with many changes in the business, with volume expansion and with two major mainframe upgrades. Only now are these systems being replaced. During the same period, stand-alone minicomputers were introduced to handle payroll/accounting ledgers, laser printing and product specifications.

1985 to Date: 3rd Generation Mainframe Systems (IBM)

Advances in technology, particularly in database management and associated software tools, led in 1983 to a reappraisal of IT strategy. A group strategy was agreed based on IBM/MVS mainframe hardware and IDMS-R software.

The current systems development plan is based on a systematic review and rewrite of 2nd generation systems into this new environment with extensive on-line facilities to provide a better service to the business and its customers. Over half the systems have been replaced in this way, including all the key database maintenance functions. The balance of systems will take a further two years to replace.

As well as mainframe developments, a policy of stand-alone mini-computers has continued with a replacement for the payroll and accounting ledger equipment. Microcomputers have blossomed in many places; a significant proportion (48 out of 80) run new systems, developed and supported by the IT department which can be considered part of the main business systems. The remainder are used for locally produced systems and/or word processing.

CURRENT SITUATION/DIRECTION

There are now computer-based systems in all the main business functions. The company is critically dependent on those systems; any significant failures could bring large sections of the day-to-day operation of the business to a halt. A contingency plan is maintained to cover the possibility of such failures.

It will be clear from the history of systems development that the current systems include a mixture of different machine environments, data management software, programming languages and development methods. The systems vary widely in age from over 18 years old to brand new.

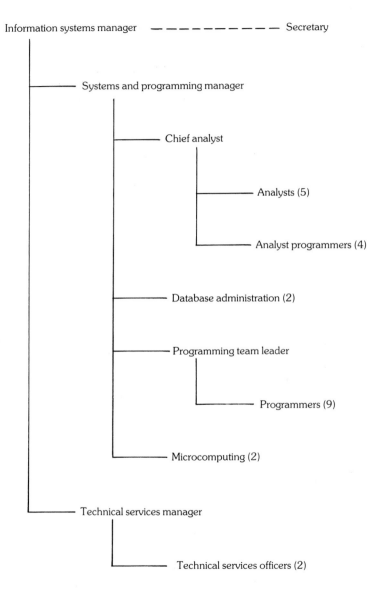

Figure A3.1 Information Systems Organisation: IS Development

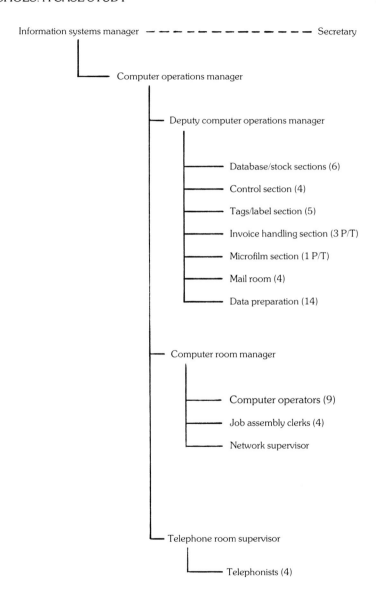

Figure A3.2 Information Systems Organisation: IS Operations

This presents two key issues to the Information Systems (IS) Department: firstly the maintenance of a wide range of skills to support the different environments and, secondly, the need for careful planning of the interfaces between old and new systems as redevelopment continues.

The organisation necessary to support current operational systems and to develop new systems is shown in Figures A3.1 and A3.2. This is a traditional structure with the IS manager reporting to a main board finance/IS director, and having functional managers reporting to him for development, technical services and operations. It is worth noting that the IS manager has acquired additional responsibilities for telecommunications, mail room and other office services in recent years. The recent selection and introduction of a digital PABX was carried out by the IS function.

Within this organisation, the Development Group uses project management and documentation standards based on Method 1; on-line systems are developed using ADS and batch processing with Cobol.

The current IT spend excluding telecommunications and office services is less than 2% of turnover. Within this environment, the preoccupations of IS management are centred on the need to:

– provide a responsive information service to companies recognising the changing pressures on:

   • central/corporate systems,

   • end-user systems including micro-based systems,

   • telecommunications and networks.

Immediate tactical concerns are to do with:

– technology

   • exploitation of current DBMS and tools,

   • identification and application of new tools as they are proven,

   • trends in hardware development, particularly onward compatibility;

– staff

   • recruitment training, re-training and retention;

- operational performance
  - security,
  - contingency planning.

Appendix 4

Sources of Information

BUSINESS INFORMATION

Anglo American Trade Directory

American Chamber of Commerce
(UK)
75 Brook Street
London
W1Y 2EB

Business Sector Surveys

Jordan & Sons Ltd
Jordan House
47 Brunswick Place
London
N1 6EE

*Britain's Privately Owned
Companies
(The Top 2000 Survey)*

Jordan & Sons Ltd
Jordan House
47 Brunswick Place
London
N1 6EE

*Business to Business
Communications*

Jordan & Sons Ltd
Jordan House
47 Brunswick Place
London
N1 6EE

The City Directory

Woodhead-Faulkner Ltd
Fitzwilliam House
32 Trumpington Street
Cambridge
CB2 1QY

Current British Directories

CBD Research Ltd
154 High Street
Beckenham
Kent
BR3 1EA

Directory of British Associations

CBD Research Ltd
154 High Street
Beckenham
Kent
BR3 1EA

Directory of European Associations

CBD Research Ltd
154 High Street
Beckenham
Kent
BR3 1EA

*Directory of Management
Consultants*

Alan Armstrong & Associates Ltd
1 Arkwright Road
Reading
Berkshire
RG2 0SQ

Directory of Management Training

Directory of Training Ltd
5–9 Headstone Road
Harrow
Middlesex
HA1 1PL

*Esprit – Performance Improvement
Training*

Esprit Ltd
Lowndes House
The Bury
Church Street
Chesham
Buckinghamshire
HP5 1HH

*Europe's 10,000 Largest
Companies*

Dun and Bradstreet International
Business Marketing Division
26–32 Clifton Street
London
EC2P 2LY

Inside Information

Alan Armstrong & Associates Ltd
2 Arkwright Road
Reading
Berkshire
RG2 0SQ

Jordan's Instant Company Index

Jordan & Sons Ltd
Jordan House
47 Brunswick Place
London
N1 6EE

Key British Enterprises

Dun & Bradstreet International
Business Marketing Division
26–32 Clifton Street
London
EC2P 2LY

Kompass

Kompass Publishers
East Grinstead House
Windsor Court
East Grinstead
W Sussex
RH19 1XD

Market Forecasts

Market Assessment Publications
2 Duncan Terrace
London
N1 8BZ

Marketing

Institute of Marketing
Moor Hall
Cookham
Berkshire
SL6 9QH

Market Location

Market Location Ltd
17 Waterloo Place
Warwick Street
Leamington Spa
Warwickshire
CV32 5LA

*Municipal Yearbook and Public
Services Directory*

Municipal Journal Ltd
178–202 Great Portland Street
London
W1N 6NH

*Sunday Telegraph UK Finance
Directory*

Graham & Trotman Ltd
Sterling House
66 Wilton Road
London
SW1V 1DE

*Trade Associations and
Professional Bodies of the UK*

Pergamon Press
Headington Hill Hall
Oxford
OX3 0BW

*The Top 3000 Directories and
Annuals*

Alan Armstrong & Associates Ltd
2 Arkwright Road
Reading
Berkshire
RG2 0SQ

Whitaker's Almanac

Whitaker
12 Dyott Street
London
WC1A 1DF

Who Owns Whom?

Dun & Bradstreet International
Business Marketing Division
26–32 Clifton Street
London
EC2P 2LY

Willings Press Guide

British Media Publications
Windsor Court
East Grinstead House
East Grinstead
W Sussex
RH19 1XC

INFORMATION
TECHNOLOGY

Association of Computing
Machinery (ACM)
c/o British Computer Society
13 Mansfield Street
London
W1M 0PB

Association of Information
Management (ASLIB)
3 Belgrave Square
London
SW1X 8PL

Federation of British
Electrotechnical and Allied
Manufacturers Association
(BEAMA Ltd)
Leicester House
8 Leicester Street
London
WC2H 7BN

British Computer Society (BCS)
13 Mansfield Street
London
W1M 0PB

British Microcomputer
Manufacturers' Group (BMME)
Owles Hall
Buntingford
Hertfordshire
SG9 9PL

British Standards Institution (BSI)
2 Park Street
London
W1A 2BS

Business Equipment & Information
Technology Association (BEITA)
8 Southampton Place
London
WC1A 2EF

City and Guilds of London Institute
46 Britannia Street
London
WC1X 9RG

Communications Users' Year Book

National Computing Centre Ltd
Oxford Road
Manchester
M1 7ED

Computer Aided Engineering,
Manufacturing & Construction
Software (Guide to)

National Computing Centre Ltd
Oxford Road
Manchester
M1 7ED

Computer Board for Universities
and Research Councils
Elizabeth House
York Road
London
SE1 7PH

Computer Peripheral Equipment
Trade Association (COMPETA)
Owles Hall
Buntingford
Hertfordshire
SG9 9PL

Computer Users' Year Book

VNU Business Publications
VNU House
32–34 Broadwick Street
London
W1A 2HG

Computer Weekly

Quadrant House
The Quadrant
Sutton
Surrey
SM2 5AS

Computing

VNU Business Publications
VNU House
32–34 Broadwick Street
London
W1A 2HG

*Computing Decisions
(Complete Guide to the Computer
Industry)*

National Computing Centre Ltd
Oxford Road
Manchester
M1 7ED

Computing Services Association
(CSA)
5th Floor
Hanover House
73–74 High Holborn
London
WC1V 6LE

Computing Services Industry
Training Council (COSIT)
Premier House
150 Southampton Row
London
WC1B 5AL

The Datacomms Book

VNU Business Publications
VNU House
32–34 Broadwick Street
London
W1A 2HG

Department of Trade and Industry
Information Technology Division
29 Bressenden Place
London
SW1E 5DT

Directory of Computer Training

Directory of Computer Training Ltd
5–9 Headstone Road
Harrow
Middlesex
HA1 1PL

The Electronic Engineering
Association (EEA)
Leicester House
8 Leicester Street
London
WC2H 7BN

IDC UK Ltd
2 Bath Road
London
W4 1LN

*Information Technology Training
Accreditation Council (ITTAC)
Register*

BCM
ITTAC
London
WC1N 3XX

Institute of Data Processing
Management (IDPM) Ltd
Henrietta House
18 Henrietta Street
London
WC2E 8NU

Institute of Electrical Engineers
(IEE)
Savoy Place
London
WC2R 0BL

*Interconnecting Applications
Handbooks*

National Computing Centre Ltd
Oxford Road
Manchester
M1 7ED

Local Authorities Management
Services and Computer Committee
(LAMSAC)
Vincent House
Vincent Square
London
SW1P 2NB

National Computer Index (NCI)

National Computing Centre Ltd
Oxford Road
Manchester
M1 7ED

National Computer Users' Forum
National Computing Centre Ltd
Oxford Road
Manchester
M1 7ED

National Computing Centre Ltd
Oxford Road
Manchester
M1 7ED

National Electronics Council
99 Gower Street
London
NW1E 6AZ

National Engineering Laboratory
East Kilbride
Glasgow
G75 0QU

National Physical Laboratory
Teddington
Middlesex
TW11 0LW

Open BTEC
Berkshire House
168–173 High Holborn
London
WC1V 7AG

Operational Research Society
Neville House
Waterloo Street
Birmingham
B2 5TX

PC Yearbook

VNU Business Publications
VNU House
32–34 Broadwick Street
London
W1A 2HG

Pedder Associates Ltd
Parkway House
Sheen Lane
East Sheen
London
SW14 8LS

Quantum Science Corporation
12–14 Denman Street
London
W1V 7RE

Science and Engineering Research
Council
Polaris House
North Star Avenue
Swindon
Wiltshire
SN2 1ET

Scottish Business Education
Council
22 Great King Street
Edinburgh
EH3 6QH

Scottish Technical Education
Council
38 Queen Street
Glasgow
G1 3DY

Software Users' Yearbook

VNU Business Publications
VNU House
32–34 Broadwick Street
London
W1A 2HG

Strategic Sales Training Ltd
Greenhill House
184 Station Road
Harrow
Middlesex
HA1 2RH

Telecommunications Engineering
and Manufacturing Association
(TEMA) Ltd
Leicester House
8 Leicester Street
London
WC2H 7BN

Who's Who in Computing

Quadrant House
The Crescent
London
SW19 8DR

Appendix 5

Manchester Polytechnic Business Skills Programme

Within the BA/BSc Business Studies Degree, the Department of Business Studies includes a business skills programme. This programme lists, classifies and develops business skills and is analogous to the training of medical practitioners: the business skills programme is to business studies as the time spent by medical students on the ward or in the operating theatre is to medical education.

The teaching process involves the definition of a range of skills and shows how they are linked together logically using the model in Table A5.1.

Increasing numbers	Mainly concerned with *people*	Mainly concerned with *processes*	Increasing judgements
	1 Self-knowledge skills 2 Interpersonal skills 3 Group working skills 4 Business social skills 5 Managerial skills	6 Communication skills 7 Research skills 8 Project skills 9 Commercial skills 10 Political and PR skills	

Table A5.1   Model of Necessary Business Skills

In detail these comprise:

1 Self-knowledge skills:

- Analysis of strengths and weaknesses;
- Setting personal goals;
- Developing personal style;
- Vision of the future;
- Proactivity – initiative;
- Energy to work;

- Enthusiasm for new ideas;
- Coping with change;
- Learning skills;
- Intuition.

2 Interpersonal skills:

- Analysis of strengths and weaknesses;
- Sensitivity to situations;
- Persuasion and motivation;
- Negotiation;
- Identification of power;
- Questioning skills;
- Effective listening.

3 Group working skills:

- Definition of objectives;
- Understanding team roles;
- Taking functional roles;
- Chairmanship and leadership;
- Group processes;
- Handling team morale;
- Handling conflict;
- Supervision;
- Liaison roles.

4 Business social skills:

- Awareness of what is appropriate;
- Non-verbal communication;
- Dress;
- Knowledge of special interest groups;
- Business ethics and morals;
- Entertaining.

5 Managerial skills:

- Power handling;
- Accountability;

- Efficiency and effectiveness;
- Planning;
- Organising;
- Controlling;
- Empathy;
- Vision.

6 Communication skills:

- Letters and memoranda;
- Minutes of meetings;
- Short action reports;
- Full business reports;
- Telephoning;
- Interviewing;
- Contributing to meetings;
- Short informal presentations;
- Formal group presentations;
- Use of visual aids;
- Verbal combat.

7 Research skills:

- Questionnaire design;
- Sample selection;
- Sources of information;
- Investigatory skills;
- Statistical analysis;
- Presentation of data;
- Drawing conclusions;
- Making recommendations.

8 Project skills:

- Defining the problem;
- Defining objectives;
- Selection of methods;
- Information collection;
- Information analysis;
- Evaluation techniques;
- Implementation;

- Control and review;
- Project management.

9 Commercial skills:

- Financial analysis;
- Commercial awareness;
- Entrepreneurship;
- Sensitivity to opportunities;
- Dealing with difficulties;
- Evaluation of risk;

- Commercial negotiation;
- Vision and originality.

10 Political and PR skills:

- Sensitivity to politics;
- Sense of presence;
- Knowledge of the media;
- Accentuating the positive;
- Writing a press release;
- Handling a media interview.

Index